Visual Basic for A-Level Computing

Bob Reeves & Dave Fogg

HODDER
EDUCATION
PART OF HACHETTE LIVRE UK

Acknowledgements

Dedicated to:

Wendy, Jack and Harry Reeves
Karen, Alice, Barnaby and Christopher Fogg

Special thanks to:

Helen Williams for all her help over the last few years, and in particular for her assistance with the second section of this book.

Graham Sparks for testing the code. You do your best work when you are supposed to be doing something else.

Every effort has been made to trace all copyright holders, but if any have been inadvertently overlooked the Publishers will be pleased to make the necessary arrangements at the first opportunity.

Although every effort has been made to ensure that website addresses are correct at time of going to press, Hodder Murray cannot be held responsible for the content of any website mentioned in this book. It is sometimes possible to find a relocated web page by typing in the address of the home page for a website in the URL window of your browser.

Hachette's policy is to use papers that are natural, renewable and recyclable products and made from wood grown in sustainable forests. The logging and manufacturing processes are expected to conform to the environmental regulations of the country of origin.

Orders: please contact Bookpoint Ltd, 130 Milton Park, Abingdon, Oxon OX14 4SB. Telephone: (44) 01235 827720. Fax: (44) 01235 400454. Lines are open from 9.00 – 5.00, Monday to Saturday, with a 24-hour message answering service. Visit our website www.hoddereducation.co.uk.

© Bob Reeves, Dave Fogg 2005
First published in 2005 by
Hodder Education, part of Hachette Livre UK
338 Euston Road
London NW1 3BH

Impression number 10 9 8 7 6 5 4 3 2
Year 2012 2011 2010 2009 2008

Typeset in 9pt Minion by Tech-Set Ltd, Gateshead, Tyne & Wear.
Printed and bound in Great Britain by Martins The Printers, Berwick-upon-Tweed

A catalogue record for this title is available from The British Library

ISBN: 9780340889213

CONTENTS

Introduction   001

Part One – Programming with Visual Basic
  1 Introduction to Visual Basic   003
  2 Project One – Text editor   010
  3 Project Two – Basic calculator   019
  4 Project Three – Car hire   028
  5 Project Four – Invoice creator   035
  6 Finding and preventing bugs   046
  7 Project Five – Jack's garage   050
  8 Project Six – Alice's chocolates   060
  9 Project Seven (Part 1) – Chris's car customiser   075
10 Project Seven (Part 2) – Chris's car customiser
   – storing and printing quotes   084
11 Project Eight – The fruit selector   098
12 Project Nine – The video hire shop   107
13 Project Ten – Alice's chocolates stock control system   117

Part Two – Coursework Projects in Visual Basic
14 Brief overview of the life-cycle of a project   125
15 Project ideas   131
16 Analysis   135
17 Overall system design   141
18 Definition of data requirements and validation   146
19 User interface design   154
20 Technical solution   158
21 System testing   160
22 System maintenance   165
23 User manual   172
24 Appraisal   176
25 Documentation needed for Module 6   179

Part Three – Appendices
  1 Code listing and forms for Section 1 Projects   183
  2 Control name prefixes   212
  3 Message boxes   213
  4 DoCmd FindRecord parameters in VBA   215

   Index   217

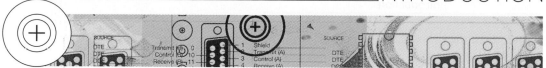

This book is designed to introduce students to programming using Microsoft Visual Basic (usually referred to as VB) and covers how to use the language for A level coursework. It is suitable for students undertaking AS and A2 computing courses.

Part One provides an introduction to VB for students who have never programmed before. It consists of practical activities to complement the theory component of your AS course and covers all of the programming techniques required at AS level. Part One also includes two chapters on using VBA within Microsoft Access.

Part Two provides guidance and advice on how to use VB to tackle the coursework element of A2 computing courses, including the selection and documentation of the project.

How to use this book

Part One introduces the key components of VB through a series of tasks. Units 1 to 11 cover VB and units 12 and 13 cover VBA in Access. There is no requirement to have studied programming before, though it is assumed that students will be covering the theoretical aspects of programming as part of their course. Students using the VBA chapters must be familiar with the process of setting up a relational database in Access.

This part of the book contains clear instructions, accompanied by screen grabs of VB, so that the student can build their programs step by step. The full code listing and completed forms for every task are shown for reference in Appendix 2.

Students should work through these tasks in order, as later tasks will require skills learnt in earlier tasks. There is one task per chapter, with each task introducing a number of VB features. Students can work at their own pace through each task either at school/college or at home. Some chapters include extension tasks. Students will find that the chapters get harder as the book progresses and that the tasks take longer to complete.

Part Two explains how to complete the A2 coursework. The chapters work through the life cycle of the project. An example project called 'Alice's Chocolates' is used to provide examples at each stage. There is also advice on how to choose your project and what documentation is required.

Visual Basic versions

All the examples used in this book are written in Visual Basic 6 but can also be implemented in version 5. It is not the intention of this book to cover VB.Net, although all the projects can be converted using the conversion facility provided by VB.Net. VBA examples are taken from Access 2000.

Conventions

In Part One, numbered text indicates an instruction for you to carry out in Visual Basic. For example:

1   Double-click on the **CLEAR** command button.

Visual Basic code is shown in a different font throughout. For example:

```
Private Sub cmdClear_Click()
  txtTextEdit.Text = " "
End Sub
```

In some cases the code is too long for the width of the book and has been split across two or more lines. Where this is the case an underscore is used. You should type this into VB as one whole line. For example

```
txtTotal.exVAT = Val(txtDayTotal)+ Val(txtkmTotal) + _
Val(txtStand)
```

If there is no underscore at the end of the line it means that it should be typed on separate lines in VB.

In Part Two, all examples are taken from the example project 'Alice's Chocolates', which is introduced in Chapter 14.

An important note for teachers and students

The example used in Part Two is designed as a means of explaining how to document a project. The problem and the solution are of an A2 standard but you should not assume that it represents any particular grade.

Different exam boards use different mark schemes and these change over time, so it is very important that you refer to the current specification from your exam board. They will also provide examplar projects at different grades.

The exam boards are well aware of support materials that are available to students, so you should not use any of the examples in this book for your own coursework.

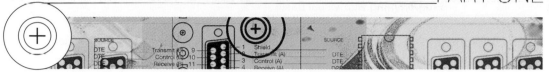

PART ONE

Programming with Visual Basic

Unit 1 Introduction to Visual Basic

BASIC is short for Beginners All-purpose Symbolic Instruction Code and, as the name suggests, it was originally designed to help students to get started with writing computer programs. BASIC was originally developed in the 1960s, but it has come a long way since those early days. The latest versions, such as Microsoft's Visual Basic, are used by professional programmers to create 'full-blown' applications.

Visual Basic is a bit of a mouthful so we will be using the term 'VB' from now on.

A VB program has two main views. The first is the lines of code, or sequences of instructions that make up your program. The computer carries out these instructions in order to perform some sort of process. The second much more modern component is the Graphical User Interface (GUI). This is what the user actually sees and uses to control the program.

The rest of this unit will be concentrating on the GUI part of a program and the specialist terms that are used within VB for these components.

Projects

VB calls each program or application you create a **project**. As you work your way through this book, you are probably going to create a lot of projects. You will probably have to produce a large project as part of the coursework element of your course.

A VB project consists of a number of **files**. Even a simple project will consist of at least three files, while the solution to a more complex problem could well be made up of twenty files or more. With so many files on the go it is a very good idea to create a new folder for each of your VB projects.

Forms

Most programmers create solutions for others to use. What these end users will see on the screen in front of them will be one or more **windows**. While you are developing your project, these windows are known as **forms**. Most major applications tend to have one main form that in turn leads to other, less important forms, known as **sub-forms**.

Classic examples of this technique include Microsoft's Word and Excel. In each case there is one main form where you enter the data, which in turn is supported by other windows that allow you to control aspects of the application. For example, you would use a sub-form to alter details of the font you want to use, or to carry out a search and replace or spell-check (see Figure 1.1).

Controls

A form is merely the backdrop. The things that do the work and display all the details and data are called **controls**. This includes things such as **command buttons**, **drop-down lists**, **button bars**, **data capture boxes** and **scroll bars**.

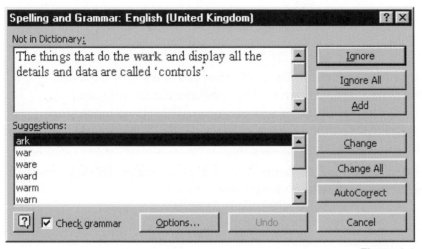

Figure 1.1

Figure 1.1 shows a typical spell-check window from Microsoft Word. Two **text boxes** contain the text that is being checked and the list of suggested alternatives, while each text box also has a **label** that tells the user what the contents of the text boxes are supposed to be. There are ten **command buttons** that make the computer do something when they are pressed, such as 'Ignore' or 'Change'. The command button in the bottom left-hand corner uses an icon, rather than words, to tell the user what it does. Finally, there is a **check box** that records whether or not the user wants the grammar checking as well.

Properties

The way a control looks and, to some extent, what it can and cannot do are controlled through its **properties**. For example, you might use properties to fix the position of a control precisely within a form. In Figure 1.1, all the command buttons down the right-hand side of the form are the same size and they are all in a neat vertical column. This can be achieved by setting the width, height and left and top **properties** of the controls.

You will notice that the 'Undo' button has been greyed out, indicating that this particular control has been disabled: clicking on it has no effect.

The 'Check grammar' check box has been set so that it is currently selected and the caption at the top of the form has been changed to tell the user what the form is designed to do. These are two more examples of how properties can be used to organise features of a control.

Methods

In order to make the program do anything, you have to tell it how to react to the user's requests. These might include dragging the slider on a scroll bar, clicking on a button, pressing a key on the keyboard or dragging an icon. These actions are all called **methods**.

By far the most common method you are likely to use is clicking on a control. However, you may also provide for double-clicking, clicking with the right rather than left mouse button or pressing a key on the keyboard.

How the program reacts to these methods will depend on what you want them to do. A click on one command button might open another window (as in the case of the spell check), while a click on another button might produce a drop-down list that the user then clicks on again, or it could close the window. All of these actions are called methods.

Enough theory – now it is time to see VB in action.

Getting started

1 Load **Visual Basic**.

2 Click on the **Standard EXE** icon (see Figure 1.2).

Figure 1.2

EXE is short for 'executable'. An executable file is another name for a program. Selecting this option means that eventually you will be able to create a stand-alone program that will not need to have access to VB itself.

3 Click on the **Open** button.

This will lead you to a screen that looks like Figure 1.3. You may find there are some other windows open already. These will be discussed later in this unit.

The Start button which executes the code you have written allowing you to see your program running.

The Stop button which stops the program running taking you back to design mode.

The View Code and View Object icons that allow you to switch between the design of the form and writing the code.

The Project Explorer window that shows all the forms and modules used in the program.

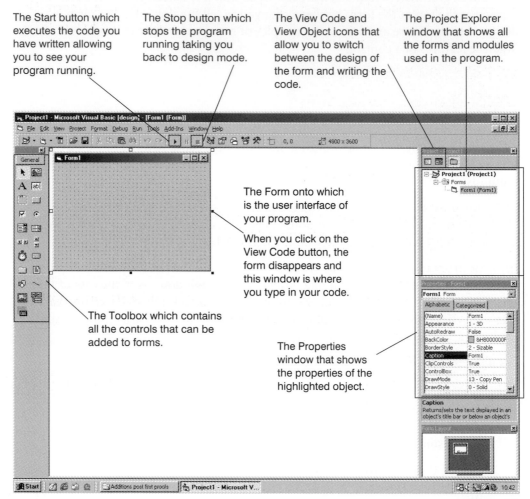

The Form onto which is the user interface of your program.

When you click on the View Code button, the form disappears and this window is where you type in your code.

The Toolbox which contains all the controls that can be added to forms.

The Properties window that shows the properties of the highlighted object.

Figure 1.3

As you can see, VB has already opened a form for you and it has been given the default name of **Form1**.

When you want to re-open the project at a later date you should do this through the folder you have set up, rather than through Visual Basic itself. This will avoid any problems of VB trying to access files that are not in the folder.

There are three sub-forms that allow you to control the forms, controls and properties that are available. Each of these sub-forms can be opened by clicking the appropriate button on the toolbar.

The Project Explorer

4   Click on the  **Project Explorer** icon.

This will open a window like that in Figure 1.4, or it may already have been open. This shows a list of all the forms and modules that are part of the current project. At the moment this shows just **Form1**.

Figure 1.4

All VB programs have two basic views when you are designing your program. These are the forms that act as an interface and the code that actually makes the program do something useful. Each form has its own code.

5   Click on the ▤ **View Code** icon.

At present Form1 has no code attached to it, but you can see the sheet where you will type lines of code that will make your programs work.

6   Click on the ▤ **View Object** icon to go
back to the form.

When you are creating programs you will be continually switching between these two views, so these two buttons are very important.

The Toolbox

7   Click on the 🛠 **Toolbox** icon.

This will open a window that shows all the controls that are currently available to you.

It is possible to add other controls, such as a **slider** or a **progress bar** to this collection. We will look at how to do that in a later unit.

You might recognise some of the controls in the **Toolbox** from other applications that you have used. We will be looking at how you use these controls in other units, but a brief summary of the more useful controls is given in Figure 1.5.

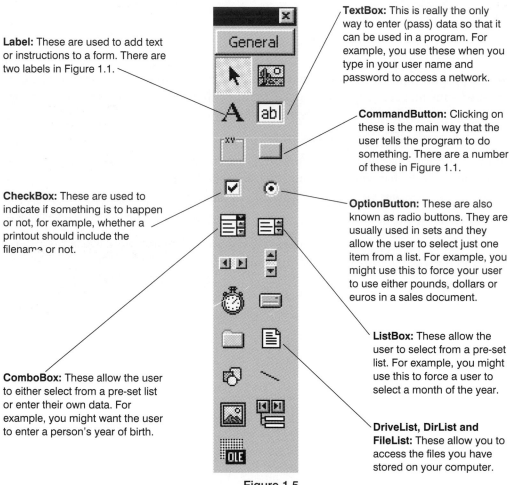

Label: These are used to add text or instructions to a form. There are two labels in Figure 1.1.

CheckBox: These are used to indicate if something is to happen or not, for example, whether a printout should include the filename or not.

ComboBox: These allow the user to either select from a pre-set list or enter their own data. For example, you might want the user to enter a person's year of birth.

TextBox: This is really the only way to enter (pass) data so that it can be used in a program. For example, you use these when you type in your user name and password to access a network.

CommandButton: Clicking on these is the main way that the user tells the program to do something. There are a number of these in Figure 1.1.

OptionButton: These are also known as radio buttons. They are usually used in sets and they allow the user to select just one item from a list. For example, you might use this to force your user to use either pounds, dollars or euros in a sales document.

ListBox: These allow the user to select from a pre-set list. For example, you might use this to force a user to select a month of the year.

DriveList, DirList and FileList: These allow you to access the files you have stored on your computer.

Figure 1.5

The Properties window

8   Click on the 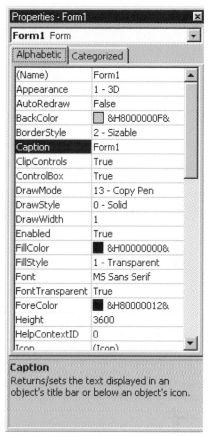 **Properties Window** icon.

This opens a window that shows the properties of the currently selected form or control. (The window may already have been open.)

You will remember that all the controls and forms you create have **properties**. These generally allow you to alter the appearance and characteristics of the currently selected form or control.

This particular window shows some of the properties of **Form1**. Some of these, such as **Font** are self-explanatory. Others, such as **Enabled** and **Height** will take a little more thought.

Each control and form has its own set of properties and we will be looking at some of the more important properties in later units.

Properties - Form1	⊠
Form1 Form	▾

Alphabetic	Categorized

(Name)	Form1
Appearance	1 - 3D
AutoRedraw	False
BackColor	&H8000000F&
BorderStyle	2 - Sizable
Caption	Form1
ClipControls	True
ControlBox	True
DrawMode	13 - Copy Pen
DrawStyle	0 - Solid
DrawWidth	1
Enabled	True
FillColor	&H00000000&
FillStyle	1 - Transparent
Font	MS Sans Serif
FontTransparent	True
ForeColor	&H80000012&
Height	3600
HelpContextID	0
Icon	(Icon)

Caption
Returns/sets the text displayed in an object's title bar or below an object's icon.

Figure 1.6

⊕ Unit 2 Project One – Text editor

Task Create an application that will allow a user to enter text (like **Notepad**). The solution must be able to clear any text that has been entered. You should be able to close the solution.

Aims Introduce the basic components of a VB project. Work with text boxes and command buttons.

Although this is a straightforward task, it is still a good idea to think about the design of the solution before you start. The specification calls for an area where the user can enter text and command buttons to clear the text and to exit the program.

Creating the form

1   Create a new folder for this project then open a new VB project. If you are uncertain how to do this then re-read Unit 1.

2   The default form (Form1) will probably be too small to show very much text, so make it larger by dragging the **handles** (the boxes round the edge of the form) until you achieve the size and shape you want (see Figure 2.1).

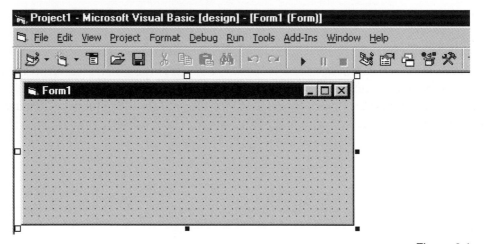

Figure 2.1

All the names given to controls (such as buttons and text boxes) that you add to a form must be unique. This is also true for the names given to each form in your project. This name cannot be used for anything else within the project. The convention is that the names of all forms should start with the prefix **frm**. A list of all the commonly used controls and their prefixes can be found in Appendix 1.

3   Unless it is already open, open the **Properties Window** by selecting **Properties Window** from the **View** menu, or by pressing F4.

The **Properties Window** shows the properties (a list of each aspect of the selected control that can be changed) of the currently selected form or control. In this case it should show the properties of **Form1**.

4   Move to the top of the list of properties and change the name of the form by altering the **Name** property.

The name should begin with the prefix **frm** and it should indicate the purpose of the form. In the example in Figure 2.2 the form has been renamed **frmMainPage**.

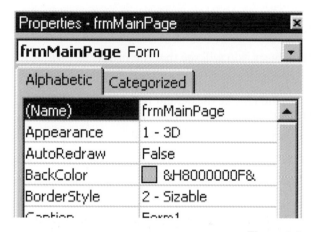

Figure 2.2

Notice how the use of capitals helps to identify the words used. You might prefer to use underscores in the name, so it might look like this: **frm_Main_Page**. You can only use letters, numbers and the underscore character in form and control names. They must, however, start with a letter. You cannot use spaces in the names you choose.

Adding a text box

We are now going to add a **text box**. This is the area where your user will enter their text.

5   Click on the **TextBox** icon in the toolbox. You may need to open the toolbox first by selecting **Toolbox** from the **View** menu.

6   Drag the mouse across the form to create a new text box (see Figure 2.3).

You can move and resize the text box using the **handles**. It doesn't matter too much if you go wrong, as you can always drag the handles to the size you want later.

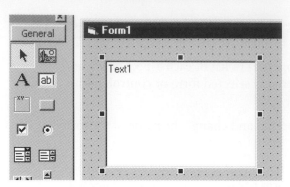

Figure 2.3

Changing properties

As the text box is the currently selected object, you will see that the properties window now shows its details.

7   Scroll to the top of the properties list and change the default name of **Text1**. Text box names should begin with the prefix **txt**. The rest of the name should help identify the purpose of the control, so this one should be named **txtTextEdit** (see Figure 2.4).

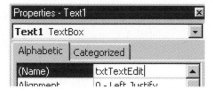

Figure 2.4

The name **txtTextEdit** is a user-defined name. Some programmers use the default names that VB provides for them such as **Form1** or **Text2**. This is not good practice because, in anything but the simplest project, you can very quickly lose track of what a control is supposed to do.

Saving the project

Having set up and renamed the form and the text box it would be a good idea to save what you have done so far. When you save for the first time, VB will ask you to save each form in your project and then ask for a name for the entire project. The form's default filename is taken from the **Name** property, but the project's filename will be **Project1** unless it is changed at this point.

8   Click on the 💾 **Save Project** icon, then locate the folder you set up earlier and save your project. Save the project as **TextEditor.vbp**.

It is up to you to decide how often you save your project, but the process is now very easy. All you have to do to save is to click on the 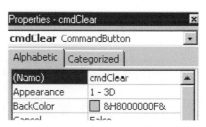 **Save Project** icon again and, just like other Microsoft products, your work will automatically be saved under the filename you chose earlier.

Adding command buttons

The specification calls for two command buttons – one to clear the text box and the other to quit or exit the program.

9 Click on the 🔲 **CommandButton** icon in the Toolbox.

10 Drag the mouse across the form to create two command buttons where you want them (see Figure 2.5).

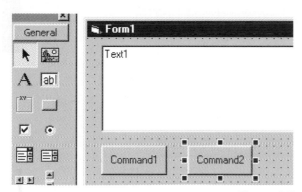

Figure 2.5

Don't be tempted to use copy and paste to create the second button – we will be looking at how to use this facility properly in a later unit. It does not matter that the captions on the two buttons are **Command1** and **Command2** — we will be changing these later. However, it would be a good idea to change the names of the two command buttons at this point.

11 Use the **Name** property to rename the two command buttons (see Figure 2.6). The prefix for a command button is **cmd**. Suitable names to use are **cmdClear** and **cmdExit**.

Figure 2.6

Tidying up the layout

Now it is time to tidy up the layout.

Make sure the command buttons and the text box are as you want them — you can resize them by dragging the **handles**.

12 Click on the form and change the **Caption** property to something more meaningful, such as **Text Editor**. The caption you enter is shown in the title bar at the top of the form.

13 Change the **Caption** property of the two command buttons to reflect their purpose, that is **CLEAR** and **EXIT** (see Figure 2.7).

You will notice that the text box already contains some text – the word **Text1** is in the top left-hand corner of the control. This text is stored in the **Text** property of the text box control.

14 Select the **Text** property and delete the existing text (see Figure 2.7).

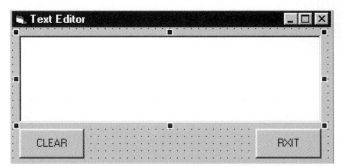

Figure 2.7

Running your program

Although your program is not yet complete it is now executable. Even though this is only a very simple program and there is little to go wrong, it is good practice to save your work before you try to execute it.

15 Click on the ▶ **Start** icon and VB will execute the program. You can also execute the program by pressing F5 on your keyboard.

Figure 2.8

You may find at this stage that your form doesn't all fit on the screen or it is off to one side. There are two ways of solving this problem.

16 Shut down your program by clicking on the ▪ **End** on the VB toolbar.

17 Click on the ⊟ **Form Layout Window** icon.

This will show where your form will appear in relation to the whole screen display when it is executed (see Figure 2.9), and you can move the form about on this window so it starts where you want.

Figure 2.9

Alternatively, if you click on the form then look at the property window, you will find a property called **StartUpPosition** and setting this to **2-CentreScreen** will do just what it says. This setting will position the form in the centre of the screen every time the form is opened.

18 Re-run your program and try entering some text.

All seems well until you try to enter text that should take up more than one line. If you want to store multiple lines of text in a text box you need to change the **MultiLine** property to **True**.

19 Close the program and then double-click the property value or select **True** from the drop-down list (see Figure 2.10).

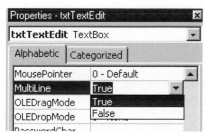

Figure 2.10

If you type in more text than the text box can hold, the text will automatically move off the top of the text box control. Although you can use the cursor keys to move up and down the text you might find it easier to set scroll bars.

20 Set the **scroll bars** property to **2–Vertical**.

21 Execute the program again.

You will notice that the scroll bar now appears. You will also find that some of the more common keyboard 'hot-keys' work. For example, you can drag over text to select it and then use CTRL C to copy, CTRL V to paste and CTRL X to cut.

Adding code

There are two final processes to carry out. The original specification asked for command buttons that would clear the text and exit the program.

22 If the program is still live then exit it.

23 Double-click on the **CLEAR** command button.

This will open a window like that shown in Figure 2.11. This window shows all the code associated with the form **frmMainPage** and positions the cursor within the section of code that is relevant to the command button you double-clicked.

You can also access the code window by clicking on the ▣ View Code icon or pressing F7.

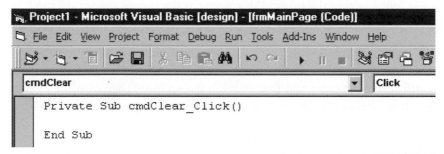

Figure 2.11

The two lines of code show the start and end of a procedure called **cmdClear_Click**. Notice how using a sensible name for the command button makes it easier to identify what the procedure is likely to do – in this case the procedure will be carried out if the command button **cmdClear** is clicked.

On the far right side of Figure 2.11 you can see the word **Click**. This shows the method that will be used to execute the code in the procedure.

In the example that you have been following, the text box that the user has been typing data into is called **txtTextEdit**.

24   In the gap between the two existing lines, key in a new line of code:

```
Private Sub cmdClear_Click()
    txtTextEdit.Text = ""
End Sub
```

Notice how the middle line has been indented. You can do this by pressing the TAB key on the keyboard. It makes the code easier to follow.

Computers are very fussy when it comes to following instructions so it is vital that you spell the control name exactly the same way you did when you originally named it.

You will notice, when typing in the above line of code, that VB displays a list of possible options after you enter the full stop character. The list is specific to the particular control you have typed before the full stop. You can either type the name of the property you wish to work with, or you can double-click its entry in the list. As we progress through this book, you may find it quicker to use the list when keying in your lines of code.

The code tells the computer to find the control called **txtTextEdit** and change the **Text** property to nothing. All data that is entered in a text box is treated as text by the program. Two pairs of speech marks with nothing between them is known as the **empty string**. This line of code tells the computer to store nothing in the **Text** property of the **txtTextEdit** control. This overwrites any text that was already in the control with nothing.

25   Return to the form design view by pressing SHIFT F7.

26   Double click on the **EXIT** command button you created earlier.

This button is supposed to exit the program – to stop it running. Clicking on the command button will add a new procedure to the code we looked at before.

27   Add the two lines of code shown below to **cmdExit_Click**. Your code should now look like this:

```
Private Sub cmdClear_Click()
    txtTextEdit.Text = ""
End Sub

Private Sub cmdExit_Click()
  Unload Me
  End
End Sub
```

28   Run your program again and test it to make sure the command buttons work as you expected.

If there are any errors in your code the program will crash and the code window will be displayed showing which line of code contains the error.

Making an executable file

If you are happy with your program you may wish to make it into a true executable. An executable is a stand-alone program — one that can be used without the support of the package that was used to create it. This means it will run on any computer even if VB is not installed on it.

29   Select **Make TextEditor.exe** from the **File** menu. You can change the name and destination folder if you want to.

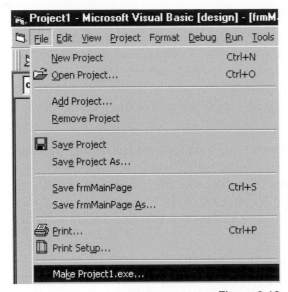

Figure 2.12

VB has now compiled your program into a stand-alone executable file.

This file can be found in the folder that contains all the other files that make up this project (unless you saved it elsewhere). Because it is now an executable, it can be transferred to another computer as a stand-alone program.

⊕ Unit 3 Project Two – Basic Calculator

Task Create an application that will act as a simple calculator. Your calculator should be able to add, subtract, multiply and divide numbers. You will also need to include a clear button.

Aims Introduce the concept of variables, assignment and declaration. Take a brief look at some basic selection.

The specification is actually quite vague – for example, there is no mention of how the numbers are to be entered in the first place. They could be typed directly into one or more text boxes, or you could use the traditional calculator approach with buttons to press that make numbers appear on a screen.

Creating the form

We are going to use the traditional calculator method. Before we start, it would be a good idea if you looked at the layout of the keys on a normal calculator. The user interface is gong to consist of a set of ten command buttons, each labelled with a digit from 0 to 9. You are also going to need another seven command buttons to cope with the four arithmetic operations ($+$, $-$, $/$, $*$), the decimal point, equals and clear. You will also need one text box that will show either the number that is currently being entered or the answer.

This task is also going to involve the creation of some code. Normally you would sort out how the code was going to work before you started the project. Planning how the code will work is just as important as planning the user interface. However, for this task we will be looking at the coding needed as and when we get to it.

Figure 3.1

1 Create a new folder and open a new VB project.

2 Add ten command buttons. As with the previous task, do not use copy and paste.

3 Name the command buttons **cmd0** to **cmd9** and change the captions as well (see Figure 3.1).

As a general rule in programming, as soon as you start repeating a process, it usually means that you should be looking for a more efficient method. This is true in this case, but the better method (called a **control array**) involves concepts that will be covered in their own right in a later unit.

Programming with Visual Basic

You can select more than one control at once by holding down SHIFT as you select each control. You will find that altering a value in the property window will affect all the controls you have selected. You could, for example, use this to ensure all the controls you have created are the same size.

4   Add suitable controls for the four arithmetic processes, the decimal point, equals and clear. Give these seven controls suitable names, such as cmdAdd and cmdequals.

5   Add a text box that will eventually act as the display 'screen'. Rename this control **txtDisplay**.

6   Change the **Text** property of this control to show a **0** rather than **Text1** and set the text to right aligned by changing the **Alignment** property of the text box.

Figure 3.2

You will notice that the title bar in Figure 3.2 has been changed by changing the caption property of the form. The minimise and maximise buttons have been removed. Figure 3.3 shows you how this has been achieved. Each form and control has a large number of properties, only a few of which we will be covering in this book. VB supplies notes on the purpose of each property and it is well worth investigating what they can do.

Properties - frmMainView

frmMainView Form

Alphabetic | Categorized

MaxButton	False
MDIChild	False
MinButton	False
MouseIcon	True
MousePointer	False
Moveable	True

Figure 3.3

Adding code for the numeric buttons

All the work you have done so far has gone into the design of the user interface, but this is only part of the solution. It is now time to consider how the program will make use of the data that your user will enter.

We will deal with the number keys first. Each time you press a number key, its value will need to be added to the right hand side of whatever is already in the text box – for example, clicking on **7** should put **07** in the text box.

7 Double click on the **1** button.

The following code will now appear. You may have used a different name for the command button(s) but the code will still be in the same format.

```
Private Sub cmd1_Click()
End Sub
```

This is an example of a procedure. The first line starts with `Private`. At this stage this has no relevance, so we can ignore it. `Sub` indicates this a subroutine – an old-fashioned name for a procedure. The `cmd1` shows which command button it is linked to and finally the `Click` tells us how the procedure is activated. The computer will carry out whatever code is placed in this procedure whenever the user clicks on the command button that has been named **cmd1**.

8 Add in the line

```
Private Sub cmd1_Click()
   txtDisplay.Text = txtDisplay.Text + "1"
End Sub
```

9 Save your project then execute it.

10 Click on the **1** button. A **1** will be added to the right-hand end of the text in the text box. The text box should now look like Figure 3.4.

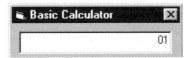

Figure 3.4

The line of code that you added takes the old value of the text property of **txtDisplay**, which was **0**, adds the character **1** to the end, then saves it back to the same text property.

In maths, an equals sign means 'is the same as', but in programming it means 'becomes'. This process is called an **assignment**.

Once you are happy with how this works:

11 Repeat the process of double-clicking on the command button then adding the line of code for the other nine numeric keys and the decimal point.

The code will be the same in each case except you will change the − "1" to the relevant number depending on the button it relates to.

As you work through this process you will need to swap between the form design and the code windows. You can use SHIFT F7 to access the form, and F7 on its own to take you to the code. The code you produce looks very repetitive. There is a more efficient way of dealing with this, but this will be dealt with in a later unit.

Adding a 'clear' button

The **clear** key uses a similar technique.

12 Double-click on the **clear** button and add the following line of code.

```
txtDisplay.Text = "0"
```

This replaces whatever was in the text box with the **0** character – effectively clearing the contents.

Using variables

There are two parts to designing a VB program – the user interface, which in this case is now complete, and the processes that will be carried out when you select a particular command button.

You need to break the processes down into a series of small instructions. You may well find that some sort of diagram helps you to understand the processes involved. These might include program flow charts, structure diagrams, and pseudo-code. In this case a simple list will do:

○ Enter the first number as a sequence of digits.
○ Click on an arithmetic key.
○ Store the first number.
○ Reset the display to zero.
○ Store the arithmetic process.
○ Enter the second number as a sequence of digits.
○ Store the second number when the equals button is pressed.
○ Carry out the calculation, using the two numbers you now have stored and the arithmetic process.
○ Display the result.

We will now deal with what happens when the user clicks on the **+** command button. The code is more or less identical for all four processes.

Before we can get started, we need to set up somewhere for the computer to store the various numbers we are hoping to work with. The numbers will be stored in what are known as **variables**. The process of creating variables is called **declaration** and it is a good idea to declare all the variables you plan to use at the start of your code.

13 Go to the top of your code and create a gap by pressing RETURN a couple of times.

14 Add in the following lines of code:

```
Option Explicit
Dim FirstNumber As Single
Dim SecondNumber As Single
Dim AnswerNumber As Single
Dim ArithmeticProcess As String
```

The `Option Explicit` forces the computer to only use variables that you have declared so, if you mis-type a variable in your program, VB will tell you.

The second line of code tells the computer to **dimension** (or set up) a variable called **FirstNumber** and that it will be a **single**. VB can store numbers in a variety of ways. A **single** is one way of storing a **real**, which means any number including decimals and negative numbers.

We need to store two numbers to add, subtract, multiply or divide, so the third line declares a variable called **SecondNumber**.

We also need to store what sort of operation has to be carried out between the two numbers. This will be stored in a variable called **ArithmeticProcess**. This data will be stored as a **string**.

Adding code for the arithmetic buttons

15 Click on the **+** key button on your form and then add the following code to the resulting procedure:

```
Private Sub cmdAdd_Click()
  FirstNumber = Val(txtDisplay.Text)
  txtDisplay.Text = "0"
  ArithmeticProcess = "+"
End Sub
```

The first line of code takes the contents of the text box (which is text) and converts it into a number using the `Val` function. This numeric value is assigned to the variable `FirstNumber`.

The second line of code resets the text box ready for the second number to be entered.

The third line of code records what sort of process we will need to carry out between the two numbers in the variable `ArithmeticProcess`.

16 Repeat this process for the other three arithmetic buttons, so that each of the four arithmetic buttons has a block of code that stores the first number, clears the text box and records what sort of operation will eventually need to be carried out.

The code will be the same in each case except you must change the "+" to the relevant sign depending on the button it relates to.

Adding code to find the answer

Finally we need to sort out what happens when the = button is pressed.

17 Double-click on the = button, then add the following code to the procedure **cmdEquals_Click**:

```
Private Sub cmdEquals_Click()
    SecondNumber = Val(txtDisplay.Text)
    If ArithmeticProcess = "+" Then
    AnswerNumber = FirstNumber + SecondNumber
    End If
    txtDisplay.Text = AnswerNumber
End Sub
```

This code works by taking the contents of the text box and storing it in the variable that was declared earlier called `SecondNumber`.

The code then goes through a selection process. In this case the equals sign is used to carry out a comparison. If the variable `ArithmeticProcess` is the + character then the variable `AnswerNumber` is assigned the value `FirstNumber` plus that of `SecondNumber`. The `End If` tells the computer where the selection process ends.

The final line of code in this procedure puts the contents of the variable `AnswerNumber` into the text box so that the user can see the answer.

Testing the program

18 Test the program by running it and entering numbers that you can easily check. Don't forget that the only button you have set up so far is the +.

There are two final steps. You need to create the code that tells the computer what to do when the −, × or / buttons are clicked. These will look very similar to the code inside the `cmdAdd_Click` procedure.

19 Double-click on each of the arithmetic process buttons in turn and copy and paste the code in, remembering to change the sign (-, x, /) in each case.

Once you have done that, you need to add three more selection processes to the `cmdEquals_Click` procedure, so that the whole routine eventually looks like this:

```
Private Sub cmdEquals_Click()
  SecondNumber = Val(txtDisplay.Text)
  If ArithmeticProcess = "+" Then
    AnswerNumber = FirstNumber + SecondNumber
  End If
  If ArithmeticProcess = "-" Then
    AnswerNumber = FirstNumber - SecondNumber
  End If
  If ArithmeticProcess = "x" Then
    AnswerNumber = FirstNumber * SecondNumber
  End If
  If ArithmeticProcess = "/" Then
    AnswerNumber = FirstNumber / SecondNumber
  End If
  txtDisplay.Text = AnswerNumber
End Sub
```

You will notice that the code has been set out so that it is easier to follow.

You now have a working solution that does all that was set out in the original specification, so you should save it and test it.

There are a number of points that need mentioning:

○ Although on the surface this task appears to be straightforward, and one that everyone can relate to, it has generated a lot of code.

○ Using user-defined names makes working with the controls and code reasonably easy. That is, naming the text box **txtDisplay** makes it easy to see what that control is for, particularly if you come back to the code at a later date, or if you are writing the program for someone else.

○ The arithmetic processes that are involved in here are simple, but breaking those processes down into small enough steps for a computer to be able to use is not always easy.

Error trapping

Although the program performs as the specification asked, there are a number of problems that are nothing to do with the specification and everything to do with the way that your program might be used.

You now have a working solution and you could decide to stop now. In fact, the job is really only half done. Unfortunately, your program is all too easy to crash or misuse.

It has been said that it takes longer to make a program truly user friendly and to 'trap' all the errors that a user might generate than it does to actually create the core processes themselves. Here are some examples of how the program could go wrong:

○ The user can enter any character they want to in the text box.
○ The user can enter the decimal point as many times as they want to.
○ After one sum has been calculated, the result is placed in the text box. Any subsequent numbers that are entered are added on to the answer from the previous question.
○ Trying to divide by zero will make the program crash.

Coping with all the errors that might occur would take a chapter all on its own and it would require a wide range of techniques. For now, therefore, we are only going to deal with the one 'fatal' error in the list.

If you try to divide a number by zero on a calculator you will get an error message. A mathematician will tell you that this is because any number divided by zero is infinity and a calculator or a computer cannot cope with the concept of infinity. If you try this with your program, you will generate what is known as a **fatal error** – an error that stops the program working altogether (see Figure 3.5).

![Microsoft Visual Basic error dialog box reading "Run-time error '11': Division by zero" with buttons Continue, End, Debug, Help]

Figure 3.5

In order to stop this happening, you need to 'trap' this error before it can do any harm. The problem is going to occur if the user has selected the division operation and the variable `SecondNumber` is zero. We need to amend the code that carries out the division process, which is in the `cmdEquals_Click` procedure.

20 Find the `cmdEquals` procedure and find the line within the procedure that is carried out when the button is pressed, then amend the code so that it now looks like this:

```
If ArithmeticProcess = "/" Then
  If SecondNumber = 0 Then
    MsgBox "You cannot divide by zero.",0,"WARNING"
    Exit Sub
  End if
AnswerNumber = FirstNumber / SecondNumber
End If
```

This algorithm now has an error trap in it. If `SecondNumber` is zero, then a message box like the one in Figure 3.6 will appear.

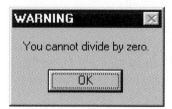

Figure 3.6

There will be more about message boxes in later units, but for now note that the `MsgBox` command is followed by three **parameters** each separated by a comma. The first is the text that appears in the box: **You cannot divide by zero**. The second, the number **0**, tells the computer what to show the user in terms of buttons to press to exit the message box. The third, **WARNING**, is the wording you want to appear in the top bar.

⊕ Unit 4 Project Three – Car Hire

Task	Create an application that will calculate the cost of hiring a car. The user must be able to see how the cost is calculated.

- ○ The cost is made up of a standing charge, a charge per day and a charge per kilometre. VAT is then added. The current rate of VAT is 17.5%.
- ○ At present, the standing charge is £10.
- ○ The charge per day is £12 for a small car, £15 for a medium-sized car, and £21 for a large car.
- ○ The cost per kilometre is 28p.

Aims Introduce labels, drop-down lists and other methods.

Creating the form

As with the previous tasks, it is important that you understand what the specification is asking for. You then need to translate this into a design. It is necessary to work out all the design details now. This includes both the GUI and how the program will operate.

As the tasks become more and more complex, it becomes increasingly important to plan first. Figure 4.1 contains all the features described in the specification.

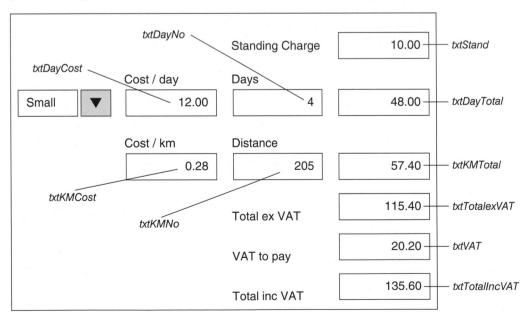

Figure 4.1

The text boxes contain some idea of the data that they might contain and all the controls have been allocated suitable names.

A number of decisions have been made about the layout:

○ All the text boxes contain numbers so they will all need aligning to the right, but units have been left out to keep it easy to follow. Note how the text boxes have been lined up.

○ A drop-down list has been used to select the car type. This means that only one car size is visible on-screen at once, again making the output clearer.

○ All the currency will be shown to two decimal places. Note that the 28p per km has also been converted to pounds to maintain the uniform appearance.

○ The number of digits that will be shown in each text box will vary, but making all the text boxes the same size makes it look organised.

○ There are two ways of carrying out the calculations – you can either include a **Calculate** button or make VB re-calculate the whole task when a key is pressed.

At this stage, you would normally go back to the user with the first draft and ask if they had a preference about the calculation method. Don't forget the solution is being created for them, not for you. We are going to use a button called **CALCULATE** because it will make the code simpler. Use the design on the previous page to help you set up the form.

1   Create a new folder, open VB and save the blank form straight away.

2   Set up the ten text boxes. The design on the previous page has been annotated to show suggested names for the text box controls.

3   Make all the text boxes the same size and don't forget to right align the contents.

4   Set the **Text** property of **txtDayCost**, **txtKMCost** and **txtStand** to **12.00**, **0.28** and **10.00** respectively.

txtkmcost and txtStand are constants – their values will not change. You should also set the **Enabled** property to **False** in each case. This would stop the user accidentally changing these values. You could also use the same technique to disable all the text boxes on the right (the ones that will contain calculations) because you do not really want your user altering these either.

5   Add labels so that the user can identify what each text box is to be used for.

You add a label by clicking on the **A** **Label** icon on the Toolbox, then dragging out roughly where you want the label to be. See Figure 4.2 for more details. You can position it more accurately later.

You change the text that is displayed in the label by changing the **Caption** property. You might find it useful to change the **AutoSize** property to **True** as well. This means the size of label will be limited by the text it contains. You should have renamed the text boxes you have already created, but in this particular case it is not necessary to rename the labels.

Adding combo boxes

6 Add a combo box by clicking on the 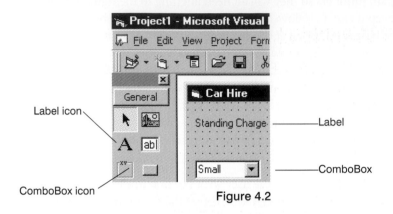 **ComboBox** icon in the Toolbox and dragging out where you want it to be.

Label icon

ComboBox icon

Figure 4.2

7 Rename the combo box as **cmbCarSize** then click on the **List** property. Enter **Small** in the box that appears and press RETURN (see Figure 4.3).

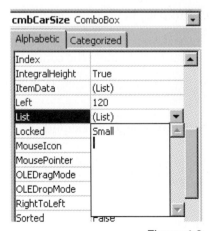

Figure 4.3

You will need to click on the **List** property twice more and enter **Medium** and **Large**. If you have to enter a long list of names, you might find it more convenient to set the list up within a text or word processor and copy and paste it in. Alternatively, if you hold down the CTRL key on the keyboard when you press RETURN, a new line is started and the box remains open, allowing you to add a new entry without needing to reopen the list.

You will notice that the text that appears in the combo box has not changed.

8 Change the **Style** property of the combo box to the **2 - Dropdown List**.

This means that the user cannot type their own text into the combo box.

9   Add a **CALCULATE** button and rename it **cmdCalculate**.

You might want to spend a few minutes tidying up the GUI at this point.

Figure 4.4

Working with combo boxes

When the program is running, the combo box will allow you to select one of the sizes on the list.

10   Ensure your program is in design view, then click on the combo box and the following procedure will be created by VB:

```
Private Sub cmbCarSize_Change()
End Sub
```

Unfortunately, this is not the way that we want the control to respond. We need to find another **method**.

11   Click on the **Procedure** box on the top right-hand side of the code screen – it will currently be displaying the word **Change**.

This list (see Figure 4.5) shows all the methods that can be associated with this particular control.

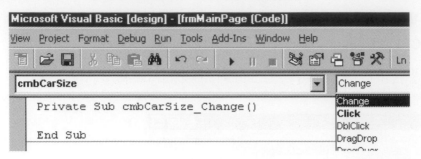

Figure 4.5

12 We want the computer to respond to a click on the combo box, so select **Click**. from the list.

13 A new procedure will now be added to the code.
    We will not be needing the first one, so delete it so that you are left with:

```
Private Sub cmbCarSize_Click()
End Sub
```

The computer will carry out this procedure whenever the combo box is clicked. When the combo box is clicked, we need the computer to make sure it is displaying the right **Cost/day**.

14 Add the following code to the procedure:

```
If cmbCarSize.Text = "Small" Then
    txtDayCost.Text = "12.00"
End If

If cmbCarSize.Text = "Medium" Then
    txtDayCost.Text = "15.00"
End If

If cmbCarSize.Text = "Large" Then
    txtDayCost.Text = "21.00"
End If
```

This code will compare the text in the combo box and if it finds a match, it will change the value in **txtCostDay**.

Even though the data we were working with is supposed to be numeric, VB treats it as text, hence the speech marks around the amounts.

Adding code to calculate the cost

You would normally sort out how the program was going to actually do anything and how it would do it as part of the design phase. However, we have left the process of calculating the cost until now.

The cost of hiring the car has three components – the standing charge, a cost linked to the number of days the car has been hired, and a third cost linked to the total distance travelled.

15 Double-click on the **CALCULATE** command button and the following procedure will be created:

```
Private Sub cmdCalculate_Click()

End Sub
```

We can find the cost for the number of days the car has been hired by multiplying the cost per day by the number of days hired.

16 Add the following line of code to the procedure to carry this out:

```
txtDayTotal.Text = Val(txtDayCost.Text) * _
Val(txtDayNo.Text)
```

Don't forget that in this book an underscore indicates that a line of code has been split to fit the page

One of the few problems with working with user-defined names is that they tend to be rather long, so lines of code do not all fit across a page. In fact, if you are using VB5 or above, you do not need to tell VB to use the **Text** property of the text boxes – it will use it by default, so this line of code could be shortened to:

```
txtDayTotal = Val(txtDayCost) * Val(txtDayNo)
```

17 Add the following four lines to this procedure to carry out the remaining calculations:

```
txtkmTotal = Val(txtKMCost) * Val(txtKMNo.Text)

txtTotalexVAT = Val(txtDayTotal) + Val(txtkmTotal) + _
Val(txtStand)

txtVAT = 0.175 * Val(txtTotalexVAT)

txtTotalincVAT = Val(txtTotalexVAT) + Val(txtVAT)
```

The first line calculates the cost of the km travelled; the next adds together the standing charge, days total and distance total, and the final two lines calculate the VAT and then add this to produce a final total due.

Formatting numbers

18 Run the program.

You will notice that as soon as you press the **CALCULATE** button, the values in the text boxes change and they lose the currency style formatting that we need.

VB supports a **format** function that allows you to control the output format in a text box.

19 Change the first line of code in the `cmdCalculate_Click` procedure to:

```
txtDayTotal = Format(Val(txtDayCost) * _
Val(txtDayNo),"0.00")
```

The format command uses the `"0.00"` to determine how to display the data. This forces VB to display at least one digit before the decimal point, even if it is zero, and it will also round the answer off to two decimal points.

20 Change the other four lines of code in the procedure so that they also use the correct format.

There is one big problem with writing a program that works this way. At some time in the future the prices are bound to go up. When they do, there is really only one solution and that is to change the values at the design stage of the program. This job can only be undertaken by someone with knowledge of VB, so your user would have to ask the programmer to create a new version. The only other alternative is to allow the user to change the values when they need to. This would mean that details of the charges would have to be held in a separate file. This will be dealt with in a later unit.

Extension tasks

1 Add a **CLEAR** button.

2 Add a combo box that allows the user to specify whether or not the person hiring the car wants insurance protection. If this is taken, it will cost an additional £20.

3 Change the distance calculation so that the rate paid per kilometre depends on the total distance: 28p per kilometre for the first 200km, then 21p per kilometre for every kilometre over 200.

⊕ Unit 5 Project Four – Invoice Creator

Task Alice's Chocolates makes and sells expensive chocolates, but only sell via mail order. They make just six different varieties, but the customers can order as many as they want of each type. Details of the chocolates they make and the prices they charge are given in the table below.

Chocolate Type	Cost each (p)
Citrus Cream	65
Toffee Swirl	54
Mint Green	37
Dark Truffle	43
Coconut Milk	76
Cherry Supreme	98

Minimum order value £8.00.
All prices include VAT

Post and Packing	£4.25

Create a program that will produce an invoice for the company to send to customers. You need to be able to print out the invoice so a copy can be included with the goods.

An invoice is a detailed receipt given to a customer by a business as proof of purchase. It itemises everything that the customer has bought, including a description. It also includes the total value of all the goods.

Aims Introduce the concept of control arrays, working with index numbers and parameters, iterative processes through For/Next loops, selection through Select/Case and simple printing.

Design

The customer can order anything between one and six different varieties of chocolate, so there will need to be six order lines that will start out blank. Each order line will show the type of chocolate, the price per chocolate, the number being ordered and the total cost for that type of chocolate.

Although the form is only going to be used by the company, it is going to be printed and sent out to the customers, so it needs to be clearly set out.

The GUI will consist of a number of text boxes for the customer details and the six order lines mentioned above. There will also need to be text boxes to store the total number of chocolates ordered and the total value of the order. These two totals are important because they can be used as a batch total and a checksum respectively.

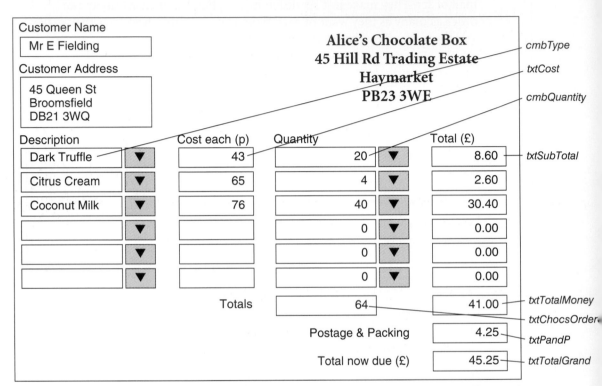

Figure 5.1

The GUI design in Figure 5.1 shows that we will be using some sort of drop-down list to select both the type of chocolates and the number required. You wil see that there is no **Calculate** button. This is because we are going to make VB recalculate whenever any of the details are changed.

The code will work as follows:

○ Identify the chocolate type selected.
○ Find the price for that type and display it.
○ Calculate the sub-total for that type of chocolate.
○ Add all the costs together.
○ Add the postage and packing.
○ Calculate the total cost.
○ Calculate the total number of chocolates being ordered.

Creating the Interface

1   Create a new folder and open and save a new VB project. Rename the form **frmInvoice**.

2   Add suitable text boxes for the customer's name and address.

The address takes up more than one line, so you will need to set the multi-line property to **True**.

3   Add a combo box and position it under the 'Description' label as shown in Figure 5.1. The one in the design is called **cmbType**. This will let the user select the type of chocolate(s) they want.

4   Enter each type of chocolate shown in the task instructions into the **List** property then set the **Style** property to **2**. This will ensure that the user cannot invent their own type of chocolate.

We are going to copy and paste in order to produce copies of this combo box.

5   Select the completed combo box **cmbType** and either click on the **Copy** icon on the screen or use the keyboard shortcut CTRL C.

6   Now paste using either the **Paste** icon or the shortcut CTRL V.

A message will appear asking if you want to create a **control array** (see Figure 5.2).

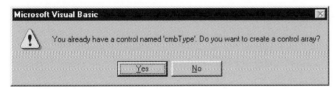

Figure 5.2

7   Click on **Yes**.

Two things will now happen. The first is that a copy of the combo box will appear in the top left-hand corner of the form (see Figure 5.3).

8   Drag this control to below the first combo box.

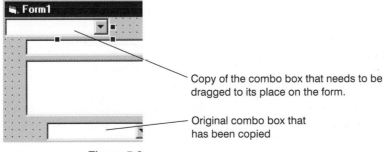

Figure 5.3

The other change is that the new combo control has been re-named for you. It will be called **cmbType(1)** (see Figure 5.4). If you click back on the original, you will find its name has been modified so that is now **cmbType(0)**.

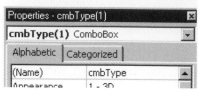

Figure 5.4

9 Paste four more copies of **cmbType**. These will automatically be named so that the last one has the name **cmbType(5)**.

10 Arrange these six controls in a column, like the one shown in Figure 5.1.

Although it may look like you now have six seemingly identical controls, the computer handles them as six parts (or elements) of the same control. This is known as a **control array** and this one is called **cmbType**. Each of the six elements is identified by an **index number** and they are numbered from **0** to **5**.

You will find that the five copies have the same properties as the original. This is fine as long as you have set the control up carefully in the first place, but it can be awkward if you find you need to correct a spelling mistake or add a new item to the list.

11 Add a text box that will (eventually) display the cost each per chocolate as shown in Figure 5.1.

For now, the text in the control should be empty but right aligned. The example in Figure 5.1 is called **txtCost**.

12 Use copy and paste to create a control array of six txtCost text boxes that will show the prices.

13 Line up the elements in the order in which they have been created.

14 Set up a combo box to show the quantity of each chocolate that has been ordered as shown in Figure 5.1. Name this control **cmbQuantity**. Set up a range of suitable quantities in the first control you create, so that these values are also used with the other elements of the control array (see Figure 5.5).

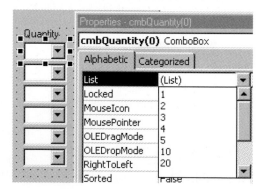

15 Copy and paste this control to create an array of six combo boxes.

Figure 5.5

Using a combo box means that the user can either choose from the list or enter their own value. Using Figure 5.1 as your template:

16 Add a text box control array to store the six sub-totals under the Total(£) label. They should be called **txtSubTotal**.

17 Add text boxes that will (eventually) store the total number of chocolates ordered, the total cost of all the chocolates, the postage and packing and, finally, a total cost. These should be called **txtChocsOrdered**, **txtTotalMoney**, **txtPandP** and **txtTotalGrand**.

18 Put the value **4.25** in the postage and packing text control. Don't be tempted to include the £ sign. If you do, the computer will not be able to evaluate the control properly.

19 Finally create a **Print Invoice** command button. Call it **cmdPrint**. Add labels to explain what all the text boxes do.

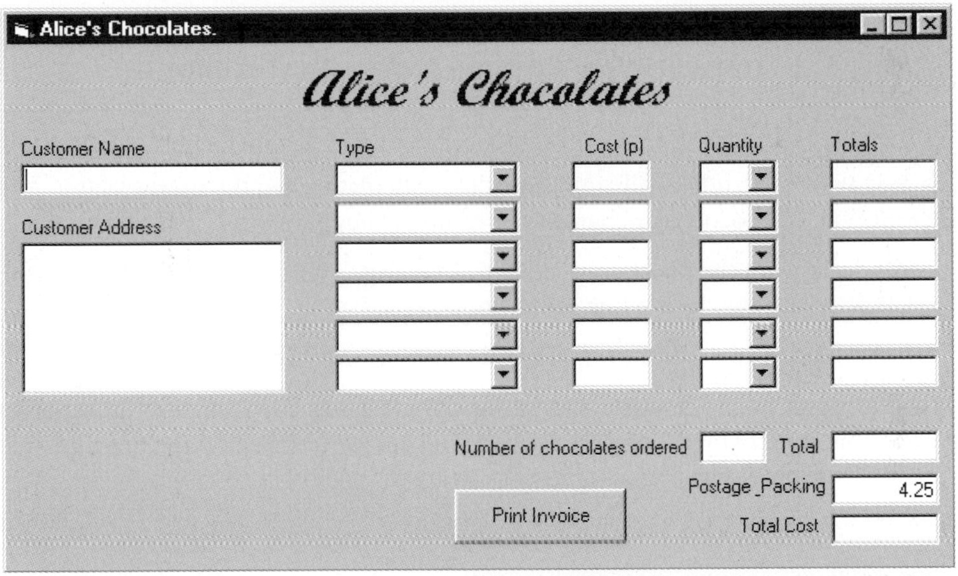

![Screenshot of the Alice's Chocolates invoice form with title "Alice's Chocolates", fields for Customer Name, Customer Address, Type, Cost (p), Quantity and Totals columns, and entries for Number of chocolates ordered, Total, Postage _Packing (4.25), Total Cost and a Print Invoice button.]

Figure 5.6

You will notice that this is not an exact copy of the original design in Figure 5.1. Designs are there to make you think and plan what you intend to do. What the project does has not changed, but the layout has. Your design will probably be different again, but this does not matter, as long as it has all the relevant features.

Creating the variables

We need to create variables that can store the total value of the order and the total number of chocolates.

20 Open the **Code Edit** view by pressing F7.

21 Add the following lines at the top:

```
Option Explicit
Dim MoneyCounter As Single
Dim ChocCounter As Integer
Dim Counter As Integer
```

This declares three variables. MoneyCounter will be used to store the total cost and ChocCounter the total number of chocolates ordered.

We will be using the variable `Counter` to act as a counter, but more about that later.

Working with control arrays

22 Move to **View Object** by pressing SHIFT F7, then double-click on **cmbType(0)**. The following procedure will be created by VB:

```
Private Sub cmbType_Change(Index As Integer)
End Sub
```

The program will work by recalculating the totals every time the user changes a value. This means that the totals will automatically recalculate when the user selects a different type of chocolate or changes the number they want.

23 We don't want the program to react to a **Change** event — we want it to react to a **Click**, so change the top line of the code to read:

```
Private Sub cmbType_Click(Index As Integer)
```

VB will respond to a wide varierty of actions or methods. You can view the actions that relate to this control by clicking on the box with the word **Click** on the top right-hand side of the screen (see Figure 5.7).

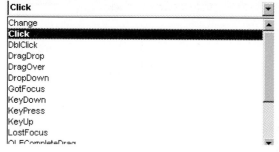

Figure 5.7

You will notice that, unlike all the other procedures we have created, this one has something inside the brackets on the end of the procedure. This means that the procedure is expecting a parameter or value that will be called `Index` and that it will be treated as an integer.

Clicking on any of the six **cmbType** controls will bring the program to this procedure. VB can indentify the particular **cmbType** you have clicked on by referring to its **Index**. The first **cmbType** will return **0**, and the last one an index of **5**.

Clicking on the **cmbType** box will normally indicate you have selected something, so we need to make the program react to this. The steps that need to be carried out are:

○ Identify the type of chocolate selected.
○ Find the price for that type and display it.
○ Display a default quantity in the **Quantity** combo box.
○ Calculate the sub-total for that type of chocolate.
○ Add all the costs together.
○ Add the postage and packing.
○ Calculate the total cost.
○ Calculate the total number of chocolates being ordered.

We can use the **Text** property of the **cmbType** control to identify the type of chocolate.

In order to find the price, we need to carry out a number of selections. For now, we will use a series of **If/Then** processes to do this.

24 Type the following series of **If/Then** commands into the procedure so that it looks like this:

```
Private Sub cmbType_Click(Index As Integer)
If cmbType(Index).Text = "Citrus Cream" Then _
txtCost(Index) = "65"
If cmbType(Index).Text = "Toffee Swirl" Then _
txtCost(Index) = "54"
If cmbType(Index).Text = "Mint Green" Then _
txtCost(Index) = "37"
If cmbType(Index).Text = "Dark Truffle" Then _
txtCost(Index) = "43"
If cmbType(Index).Text = "Coconut Milk" Then _
txtCost(Index) = "76"
If cmbType(Index).Text = "Cherry Supreme" Then _
txtCost(Index) = "98"
End Sub
```

25 Save the project and execute it.

26 Click on one of the **cmbType** controls and select a type of chocolate.

You will find that the appropriate price appears alongside the control you are working with, and that the price changes when you select a new type.

There are, however, some problems with using multiple **If/Then** statements like this. Firstly it is repeating the same process six times over and, secondly, you can enter whatever you like in the **cmbType** boxes and the box will store the text and retain the old cost.

Using a Case statement

An alternative to using **If/Then** constructs is to to use a **Case/Select** contruct.

27 Delete the six **If/Then** statements and instead enter:

```
Select Case cmbType(Index)
 Case "Citrus Cream": txtCost(Index) = "65"
 Case "Toffee Swirl": txtCost(Index) = "54"
 Case "Mint Green": txtCost(Index) = "37"
 Case "Dark Truffle": txtCost(Index) = "43"
 Case "Coconut Milk": txtCost(Index) = "76"
 Case "Cherry Supreme": txtCost(Index) = "98"
 Case Else: txtCost(Index) = ""
End Select
```

This process works by comparing the value after the `Select`. It works in almost the same way as the **If/Then** code you deleted. The final `Case Else` statement tells the computer what to do if none of the selections match up. In this case, that would be if the user had typed in a type of chocolate that was not on the list. The code puts the empty string in the appropriate cost control.

Adding code to calculate the cost

Now we need to find the total cost for the type that has been changed.

28 Add the following line after the **Select Case** process:

```
txtSubTotal(Index) = (Val(txtCost(Index)) * _
Val(cmbQuantity(Index))) / 100
```

This one line will calculate the cost of any of the six order lines that you are currently working on. It uses the value of `Index` to decide which order line it needs to calculate. The `/100` converts the value into pounds rather than pence.

Finding total cost seems like a simple process. One way to find the total is to add together the values held in `txtSubTotal(0)`, `txtSubTotal(1)`, `txtSubTotal(2)` and so on. In this case, there are only six elements in the array, so this method might just about be practical. However, this is another example of repeating a process, so we should look for a better method.

A more efficient method is to use an **iterative process**. This is also known as a **loop**. In this case, we will be using a **For/Next** loop.

29 Add the following five lines of code:

```
MoneyCounter = 0
For Counter = 0 To 5
MoneyCounter = MoneyCounter + Val(txtSubTotal(Counter))
Next
txtTotalMoney = MoneyCounter
```

The first line sets an accumulator called `MoneyCounter` to 0. This variable will keep a running total of the cost of the chocolates for us. If you don't set it to zero the grand total will keep on increasing every time you change a value.

The second and fourth lines define the iterative process. An iterative process is one that is repeated a number of times. In this case the value of `Counter` is set to 0 by the line `For Counter = 0 to 5`.

When the program reaches the `Next` it returns to the `For` line and `Counter` increases by 1 to 1. When `Next` is reached the next time, it returns to the `For` line again and `Counter` increases to 2 and so on until `Counter` becomes 5. This time when it reaches the `Next`, it just carries on (rather than going back to the `For` line). To put it simply, you have set up a process that counts from 0 to 5, and it is `Counter` that is doing the counting.

The line inside the iterative loop takes the value held in each successive `txtSubTotal` element and adds its on to the accumulator so, the first time through, it adds `txtSubTotal(0)` to `MoneyCounter`. Next time it adds on `txtSubTotal(1)` and so on.

The last line of the this block of code puts the total value of the order in the appropriate text box.

30 Add the following line to the end of the procedure:

```
txtTotalGrand = val(txtPandP) + Val(txtTotalMoney)
```

This adds the cost of the postage and packing (set at 4.25) to the cost of all the chocolates and shows the total cost of the order. You might want to try adding a £ sign to the **4.25** in the postage and packing text box. You will find the program now ignores the value. This is because it cannot evalaute the £ sign, so it gives in and sets it to zero.

Adding code to count up the number of products sold

We need to add up the total number of chocolates being ordered.

31 Add the following lines to the end of the procedure:

```
ChocCounter = 0
For Counter = 0 To 5
ChocCounter = ChocCounter + Val(cmbQuantity(Counter))
Next
txtChocsOrdered = Val(ChocCounter)
```

This works in a very similar way to the algorithm that added up the total value of the order.

By now, you have probably identified a fundamental problem with the program. The calculations are only carried out if you select the number of chocolates you want first and then the type.

32 Put the program into **Edit** mode and then double-click on one of the **cmbQuantity** controls. The following procedure will be added to the code:

```
Private Sub cmbQuantity_Change(Index As Integer)
End Sub
```

33 Change the **Change** to a **Click** so that it looks like this:

```
Private Sub cmbQuantity_Click(Index As Integer)
```

What we really want the program to do now is to carry out exactly the same processes it does when you click on a **cmbType** combo box. One solution would be to copy and paste all the lines of code you have typed in already, but this means that any alterations or corrections you have to make will have to be made twice, and it will also make the program longer than it really needs to be. Remember, if you are about to copy lines of code, there is almost certainly a better method. In this case the solution is both simple and elegant.

34 Add the following single line of code to the new procedure:

```
Call cmbType_Click(Index)
```

This single line tells the computer to carry out the procedure **cmbType_Click**. Putting the variable **Index** in the brackets tells the computer which order line to work on. This is a simple example of passing a parameter from one procedure to another.

Formatting numbers

As you try out various combinations of numbers you will notice that the format of some of the answers changes. In particular, the subtotals for each of the six types will alter as the number of digits after the decimal point varies.

You can fix the output format by using a **Format** function.

35 Find the line:

```
txtSubTotal(Index) = Val(txtCost(Index)) * _
Val(cmbQuantity(Index)) / 100
```

and change it to:

```
txtSubTotal(Index) = Format(Val(txtCost(Index)) * _
Val(cmbQuantity(Index)) / 100, "0.00")
```

The **0.00** forces the result to be displayed to two decimal points.

36 Add the **Format** function to the lines that calculate txtTotalMoney and txtTotalGrand.

Printing the invoice

The last feature we have to deal with is printing the form.

37 Double-click the PrintInvoice button. The following procedure will be added to your code:

```
Private Sub cmdPrint_Click()
End Sub
```

38 Add the following lines:

```
cmdPrint.Visible = False
  frmInvoice.PrintForm
cmdPrint.Visible = True
```

This is a crude but effective way of printing. However, you really do get exactly what you see on the screen. In fact, only the middle line does the printing. You might want to work out for yourself what the outer two lines do.

Extension tasks

1 Add a **Clear** button.

2 The specification mentions that the minimum order is £8. Add code that checks for orders under £8 and brings up a suitable error message.

⊕ Unit 6 Finding and preventing bugs

This unit is slightly different to the ones you have read so far. Rather than taking you through a task, it introduces various techniques that you can use to prevent, find and correct bugs in your program. The examples used in this unit are based on the program created in Unit 5.

A bug is any error in a program that stops it working the way you want it to. Debugging is the process of finding and correcting these errors. As you begin to create more complex programs, the time you spend debugging is bound to increase. There are a number of useful debugging techniques available in VB and this unit will tell you about the main ones.

Prevention is better than cure, and there are things you can do to prevent errors creeping in. Careful planning can help and this includes sorting out suitable names for all the forms, controls and variables you intend to use before you start coding.

Option explicit

You should always use **Option Explicit**. Using this as the first line of code means you must declare all the variables you intend to use. If you mis-type a variable name or try to introduce one that has not been declared, an error message will stop you going any further (see Figure 6.1).

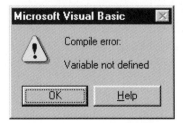

Figure 6.1

If you use this technique, then VB will highlight where the error has occurred:

```
Moneyounter = 0
For Counter = 1 To 5
MoneyCounter = MoneyCounter + Val(txtSubTotal(Counter))
Next
```

Figure 6.2

Breakpoints

You can make a program stop at any point in the code by using a **breakpoint**. You add these to your code by either clicking in the grey bar to the left of the code or pressing F9. The breakpoint shows up as a brown circle and the line of code next to the symbol will also turn brown.

```
MoneyCounter = 0
For Counter = 1 To 5
MoneyCounter = MoneyCounter + Val(txtSubTotal(Counter))
Next
```

Figure 6.3

When you execute the code and the program reaches this point, it will stop before it executes that particular line which will now be highlighted in yellow.

```
MoneyCounter = 0
For Counter = 1 To 5
MoneyCounter = MoneyCounter + Val(txtSubTotal(Counter))
  MoneyCounter = 0
```

Figure 6.4

You can now find the values held by variables and controls by hovering the mouse pointer over any occurrence of the variable or control within the program (see Figure 6.4).

You can also interrogate the program by using the **Immediate** window. If this is not visible, you can access it via the **View** menu.

To find the value of a variable enter **?** followed by the variable name (see Figure 6.5).

```
Immediate
 ?MoneyCounter
  0
```

Figure 6.5

Single stepping and variable watching

You can **single step** through the code by pressing F8. This executes each line of code one at a time. If you have a rough idea where a fault is in your code, you can single step and check the values of the variables and controls as you go.

Expression	Value	Type
moneycounter	7.35	Single

Figure 6.6

You can also **watch** a variable by selecting **Add Watch** from the Debug menu. Enter the variable name in the resulting window. This process allows you to **watch** what is happening to the variables you have declared while you single step through your code.

Once you have finished trying to find the error, you can continue the program by clicking on the **start** symbol on the button bar.

Commenting code

Lines that you suspect are causing problems can be **commented out**. Go to the start of the suspect line and add an apostrophe. When you move away from the line it will go green. This indicates that VB is now treating this as a comment and, as such, it will be ignored when the code is executed (see Figure 6.7).

```
MoneyCounter = 0
For Counter = 1 To 5
'MoneyCounter = MoneyCounter + Val(txtSubTotal(Counter))
Next
```

Figure 6.7

Errors don't always occur where VB says they are. Missing the second part of an iterative process such as a **For/Next** loop or forgetting to add an **End If** to complement an **If/Then** statement can often lead to unforseen consequences.

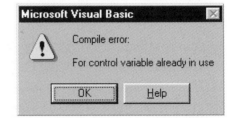

Figure 6.8

The error in Figure 6.8 was caused by a missing `Next` command in Figure 6.9. VB has identified the error in one place in the code, but the problem actually lies elsewhere.

```
MoneyCounter = 0
For Counter = 0 To 5
  MoneyCounter = MoneyCounter + Val(txtSubTotal(Counter))

txtTotalMoney = MoneyCounter
txtTotalGrand = Val(txtPandP) + Val(txtTotalMoney)

ChocCounter = 0
For Counter = 0 To 5
  ChocCounter = ChocCounter + Val(cmbQuantity(Counter))
Next
```

Figure 6.9

As you work your way through your code you should add suitable comments to indicate what each part does.

Naming conventions and formatting

You should use sensible names for your forms, controls and variables and use capital letters at the start of the words that form the names. For example, a text control should be called **txtEnterCost** rather than **txtentercost**.

When you type in the control name as part of your code, enter it all in lower case. When you move off that line of code VB will convert the name to the same format you started with so that any names that VB does not recognise will be left in lower case.

You can also make use of various formatting techniques to make your code easier to follow and therefore easier to debug. The code in Figure 6.10 has been split up by leaving a blank line between the lines of code and the contents of the **For/Next** loops have been tabbed in.

```
' add up the subtotals for each of the types
MoneyCounter = 0
For Counter = 0 To 5
   MoneyCounter = MoneyCounter + Val(txtSubTotal(Counter))
Next

' display the total owed and add on P&P
txtTotalMoney = MoneyCounter
txtTotalGrand = Val(txtPandP) + Val(txtTotalMoney)

' find the total number of chocolates being ordered
ChocCounter = 0
For Counter = 0 To 5
   ChocCounter = ChocCounter + Val(cmbQuantity(Counter))
Next
txtChocsOrdered = Val(ChocCounter)
```

Figure 6.10

The hardest errors to detect are those that are there because you have made a mistake with your logic. For example, you might check for **Yes** when the program is using **yes** or you might add two variables rather than multiplying them.

The importance of testing

Just because a project seems to be working as you would expect it to does not necessarily mean that it is. You should ensure that you test every aspect of your project as thoroughly as possible as you go along. Bugs detected at this stage will be easier to sort out than when they are part of a much bigger project. However, this does not mean that you should not test the project as a complete solution as well.

⊕ Unit 7 Project Five – Jack's Garage

Task   A small local garage wants to keep track of the work it carries out on all the cars that pass through its doors. They currently use a card index system. Once a job has been completed the mechanic finds the relevant card and adds the date and a brief description of the work that has been carried out.

Your task is to create a computer-based system that will allow the people working in the garage to add details of work that has been carried out on a car, and also to interrogate the system to find all the details for a given car.

Aims   Introduce multiple form projects. Investigate serial file handling.

Designing the solution

We will have to use some sort of file to store all the details about the cars and their repairs. There are two reasons for this:

○ The first and most important reason is that we cannot store data that either needs to be changed or will be added to as an integral part of a program or its code. This is because every time you execute the program, it starts up in exactly the same state as when you originally created it.

○ The second reason for using a file to store the cars' histories is that the file is likely to get very large. The user has not asked you to set up any routines either to delete or archive old data, which means that once car details are added they will stay in the file forever. Over a period of time this file will get very large and much of the data will be out-of-date. This is one of the points you might raise with the user, but at the moment this file is going to carry on growing for the foreseeable future.

We are going to create a simple serial-file-handling program. A serial file is a collection of records that aren't stored in any particular order. This problem lends itself to a serial file. The amount of data that is stored about each job will vary in length. There is no need to store all the details about one car together in one place – the search process will put them all in one place anyway.

As with the previous tasks, it is very important to sort out what the solution will look like and how it will work now, rather than trying to design as you go along. The use of a serial file adds another dimension to the design process, as you now need to work out the record structure you will be using within the file.

Designing the record structure

Each job carried out at the garage will make up one record in the serial file. New records will be appended to (added to the end of) the file.

There are lots of details that could be stored for each job – for example, the name of the mechanic who carried out the work, the time the job took, the cost of the parts that were used and so on. The specification states that they only want to store the date and details of the work that has been carried out.

We will also need to store the car's registration number so that the user can identify all the work that has been carried out on one given car. This means that each record will consist of three fields. Here are two typical records:

> 23/6/04
> AS 53 WAS
> Replace faulty starter motor
>
> 24/6/04
> ER 01 ABC
> Repair broken door mirror.

Because we will be working with a serial file we do not need to worry about the total amount of space each record will take up. In fact, we will be using a variable record length to store details of the work carried out.

Designing the processes

There are two basic processes – adding new records and interrogating the file.

The steps needed to add a new record are as follows:

- Enter the date (this could be done using the computer's built-in clock).
- Enter the car's registration number.
- Enter the repair details.
- Check there is data in each of these three fields.
- Append the details to the serial file.

Interrogating the records for all the details of a given car will involve the following:

- Enter the registration of the car we want to know about.
- Read each record from the file in turn.
- If there is a match, add the details to a screen display.
- Repeat this process until there are no more records to look at.

As the program progresses there will be various items of data that will need storing. There are two areas we can use to do this. Some data can be 'stored' on-screen in the various controls we are using – for example, the car's registration number. Other data cannot be stored in controls. For example, when the program reads the date from the file, there will be nowhere for it to be displayed on the screen, so we will need to create a variable, in which to store this data.

Designing the interface

There are two distinct parts to this task – adding new records and interrogating. So it would make sense to use two different forms.

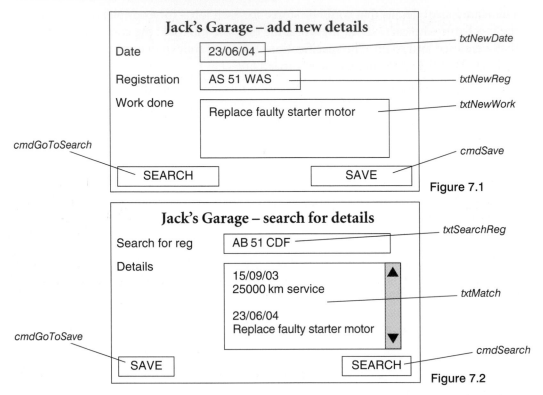

Figure 7.1

Figure 7.2

Even though both forms have a **SEARCH** and a **SAVE** command button, you should note that they will have different names. This will make following any code easier. Both the big text boxes will need to have the **multi-line** property set to **True**, and they will both need vertical scroll bars.

1   Create a new folder and open a new VB project.

2   Create and save the **add new details** form as described in Figure 7.1 as **frmNewDetails**.

We now need to create a new form for the search details:

3   Select **Add Form** from the **Project** menu, then select **Form** and finally click on **Open**. A new blank form will now be ready for you to use.

4   Rename and save the second form, which should be called **frmSearch**.

If you create a project that involves multiple forms then the computer will need to know which form to open with when the program is executed. The default form will be the first one you created: in this case, frmNewDetails.

5   Select **Properties** from the **Project** menu.

6   Under **Startup Object**, select the form that you want to appear at startup (see Figure 7.2).

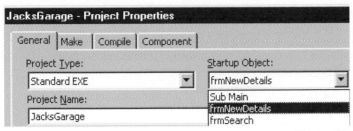

Figure 7.3

Adding the code

We are going to create the code attached to **frmNewDetails** form first. It is sensible to work on this form first. Once this has been done, we can use it to create test data for the search routine in the second form.

7   Select **frmNewDetails** in the Project Explorer window, double-click on the **SAVE** command button on the **frmNewDetails** form. The following procedure will be created.

```
Private Sub cmdSave_Click()
End Sub
```

We need to make sure that there is something in each of the three text boxes before we can save.

8   Add the following four lines of code to the procedure:

```
If txtNewDate = "" Then
  MsgBox "You must enter a date", 0, "Error"
  Exit Sub
End If
```

9   Run the program and click on **SAVE** straight away. The following error message will appear:

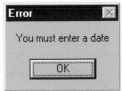

Figure 7.4

The code you have entered checks the contents of `txtNewDate`. If it is empty then the error message is displayed. The `Exit Sub` forces the computer to exit from the procedure at this point. The `End If` shows the computer where to go if the condition is not true.

10 Add similar conditions to make sure the user has typed in a registration number and details of the work done.

These are both text fields, so you can't do much more than check to make sure that something has been typed into these controls.

Saving data to a serial file

If you have entered data in all three text boxes then the program can now save the details to the file.

11 Add the following five lines after the three check routines:

```
Open "CarHistory.txt" For Append As #1
   Print #1, txtNewDate
   Print #1, txtNewReg
   Print #1, txtNewWork
Close #1
```

The first line tells the computer to open a file called **CarHistory** and gives it the file extension **txt**. Using this file extension means you can load the file into a word processor or a text editor if you want to.

If the file **CarHistory** does not already exist then a new file with this name will be created. If it does exist then anything sent to the file will be appended (added to the end of the file).

Each file you open has to have an identifier. In this case we have used number 1, but it could just as easily have been 2 or even 222. The file identifier means you can have more than one file open at one moment in time, each with its own unique identifier. However, in practice, you should close down files when you are not using them if you can.

The final line of code does just that – it tells the computer to close down the file associated with identifier 1. It also releases the identifier so that it can be used with other files if necessary.

The middle three lines of code print the contents of the three text boxes to the file associated with file identifier 1.

The final step is to clear the **reg no** and **work done** text boxes. We need to do this to stop the user inadvertently clicking on the **SAVE** button twice, but it also clears the form ready for details of another job to be entered.

12 Enter the following two lines of code after those you just entered:

```
txtNewReg = " "
txtNewWork = " "
```

Before you try this out you need to tell VB whereabouts in the directory structure it is. The simplest way to do this is as follows.

13 Save your project, exit from it, and then reload your project from the folder you created.

This process has the effect of resetting the path name for the folder.

14 Run the program, enter the details of a job and click on the **SAVE** button.

15 Close the program and find the file **CarHistory.txt**.

It should be in the same folder as the files that make up the project.

16 Open the **CarHistory** file and you will find something like this:

Figure 7.5

Adding the date

It would be very useful if the computer could put today's date in the appropriate box.

17 Double-click on the form **frmNewDetails**, but not on one of the controls. A new procedure called **Form_Load** will be created:

```
Private Sub Form_Load()

End Sub
```

Form_Load is a special procedure. The commands it contains are only carried out once – when the form is opened for the first time. We are going to use this to put today's date in the txtNewDate control.

18 Add the following line to the Form_Load procedure:

```
txtNewDate = Date
```

This makes use of a built-in VB function called Date. You will sometimes find that VB will not allow you to use certain names for your variables, forms or controls. This will probably be because the name you are trying to use is a **reserved name** – it already does something in VB. Date is an example of a **reserved name**.

Moving between forms

The project consists of two forms, so we need to set up a method that will allow us to switch between the two.

19 Double-click on the **SEARCH** command button in **frmNewDetails** and add the four lines shown below:

```
Private Sub cmdGoToSearch_Click()
   frmSearch.Show
   frmNewDetails.Hide
End Sub
```

The lines of code in this procedure reveal the form `frmSearch` and then hide the form `frmNewDetails`. Note that `frmNewDetails` has not been removed – it has just been hidden so the user cannot see it.

We now need to sort out the code that is attached to the **Search** form. You can access the **Search** form by opening the **Project Explorer** and double-clicking on the appropriate form (see Figure 7.6).

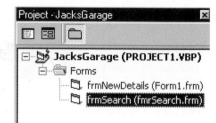

20 Double-click on the **SAVE** command button in frmSearch and add appropriate code that will take the user back to the search form. You will need to hide `frmSearch` and show `frmNewDetails`.

Figure 7.6

Adding the code for the search form

We need to create three variables to store the data that is input from the file.

21 Open the code design view for `frmSearch` and add the following four lines to the very top of the code:

```
Option Explicit
Dim InputDate As String
Dim InputRegNo As String
Dim InputText As String
```

These three variables will be used to store details from the file so they can be checked to see if they match the search criteria.

We now need to create the code that will find all the matches for a registration that is entered into the control `txtSearchReg`.

22 Double-click on the SEARCH button. This will create a new procedure:

```
Private Sub cmdSearch_Click()
End Sub
```

23 Add the following lines of code to this procedure:

```
Open "CarHistory.txt" For Input As #1
Do
Input #1, InputDate
Input #1, InputRegNo
Input #1, InputText
If InputRegNo = txtSearchReg Then
    txtMatch = txtMatch + InputDate + vbCrLf + _
    InputText + vbCrLf
End If
Loop Until EOF(1)
Close #1
```

There is a lot going on in these few lines. The first line tells the computer to find the file and open it so that data can be input from it:

```
Open "CarHistory.txt" For Input As #1
```

CarHistory is a serial file, so the computer will start with the first record and, each time you request more data to be input from the file, the computer will take whatever it finds next, whether it is what you want or not.

Using a Do / Loop Until process

We now need to repeat the process of reading in a record from the file, checking for a match, then going back and reading another record and checking for a match until there are no more records.

We have used a **Do / Loop Until** process to do this. The Do on the second line is the start of this **iterative** process. The line: Loop Until EOF(1) is the other end of the process. This sets a condition that defines when the computer can exit the loop and carry on with whatever code comes next. In this case, the computer will keep on repeating the process inside the **Do / Loop** construct until it reaches EOF(1). This acronym is short for **End Of File 1**.

There are two parts to the code inside the **Do / Loop** process:

○ The first three lines read (or input) a record from the file linked to file identifier number 1. The details are then stored in the variables you set up earlier.
○ The **If / Then** compares the car registration you have entered in the text box txtSearchReg with the registration number it has just taken from the file, which is stored in InputRegNo. If a match is found then the program adds the date and work done (which are currently stored in the variables InputDate and InputText) to the text box txtMatch.

There are two rather strange looking values in this line. `vbCrLf` is short for **VB Carriage Return / Line Feed**. It forces the computer to move to the start of a new line in the text box before adding any more text to the text box. Try removing them from your code and looking at the results of a successful search.

We have three program constructs in use: **The Do / Loop Until** loop is contained inside the **Open file / Close** routine and inside the **Do / Loop Until** is an **If / Then** selection process. This concept of fitting one construct inside another is called **nesting**. Nesting is more usually applied when similar constructs are fitted inside one another.

Before you can test this properly, you may need to go back to **frmNewDetails** and enter a number of jobs, some of which need to be for the same vehicle.

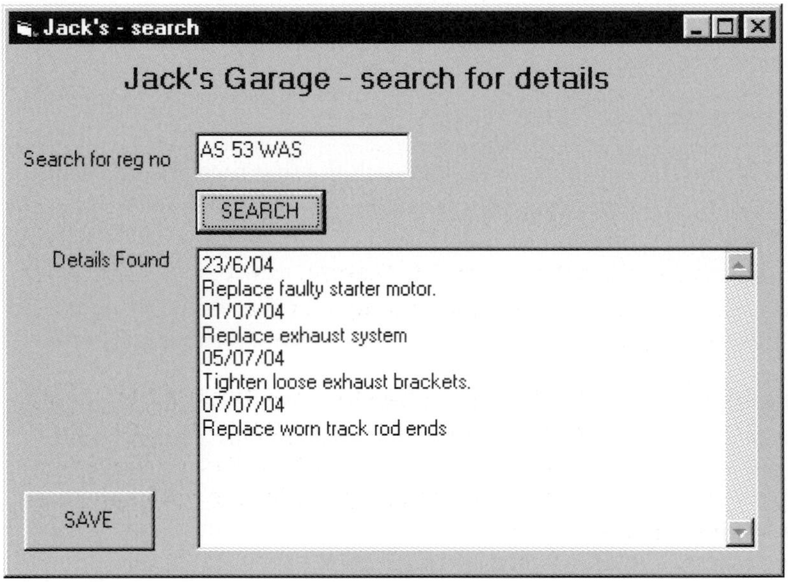

Figure 7.7

Tidying up

It is almost impossible to cover everything you need to do at the design stage of a project. There are bound to be problems that you will not have foreseen, and some of these will only come to your notice once you start using the program. There is one important thing that we should do in order to tidy up in this project.

24 Run the program and go to the **search** form.

25 Type in a valid registration number and click on the SEARCH button twice.

You will notice that the same information has now appeared twice in `txtMatch` (see Figure 7.8). This is because we have not told the program to clear the `txtMatch` control before starting a fresh search.

Figure 7.8

26 Exit the program and double-click on the **SEARCH** command button and add the following line of code to the very beginning of the procedure:

```
txtMatch = ""
```

The procedure should now look like this:

```
Private Sub cmdSearch_Click()
txtMatch = ""
Open "CarHistory.txt" For Input As #1
```

The new line sets the text property of the `txtMatch` control to the empty string. It has an added benefit in that if you enter a registration number that does not exist in your file, then the control will stay empty.

There is a fine dividing line between tidying up a program and adding in new functionality. It is all right to make a program easier to use, but there is little point straying far beyond the specification and objectives that you have agreed with the intended user. You could end up spending hours creating solutions to problems that the user wasn't really worried about anyway.

Extension tasks

1 Add a new search facility that will allow the user to find all the work carried out on a given date.

2 Add a print button that will allow the user to print details of all the work carried out on a car.

⊕ Unit 8 Project Six – Alice's Chocolates

Task Following the success of the order form system we set up for Alice's Chocolates in Unit 5, they have asked you to set up a stock control system:

○ They want to be able to enter the number of each type of chocolate that has been ordered by a customer into a system that will keep track of how many chocolates they have left in stock.

○ They want the system to automatically tell them when their stock has dropped below a set level. This restock level is likely to be different for each of the six types of chocolate they make, because some types are more popular than others.

○ They also want to be able to change this restock level if they need to because they do not want to have excessive numbers of chocolates in stock. They have no plans of making more than six different types of chocolate.

○ These are the current stock and restock levels:

Chocolate type	Current stock level	Initial restock level
Citrus Cream	234	200
Toffee Swirl	560	400
Mint Green	455	450
Dark Truffle	459	300
Coconut Milk	354	250
Cherry Supreme	250	100

Aims Introduce user-defined data types, random access files and more on message boxes. Using tab stops to navigate around forms.

At this point in time, Alice's Chocolates has made no mention of integrating this task with the invoice system you set up in Unit 5. They want this to be set up as a stand-alone system. In the long run, this is likely to be expensive, but you must remember that in the end, the solution is to suit the users', not yours.

Design

The data we are going to store will always be changing, therefore we need to store it in some sort of file that the program can access. In this case we need to store the type, current stock and restock levels. Note that we have not been asked to store details of previous transactions.

A random access file uses a system of reference numbers to allow the user to jump straight to the record they want. This task is well suited to this approach. Although random access files are more complex to work with than the serial file we used in the previous unit, they are also a lot more versatile. The main characteristic we will be using is that when you update a random access file, you overwrite whatever data is already there – there is no need to create a whole new record.

The solution needs to be able to carry out the following processes:

○ Store the details for six types of chocolate. There is no indication that the user wants to store more than six.
○ Change the current stock level, restock level and the type of chocolate.
○ View the current stock levels.
○ Decrease the stock levels as chocolates are sold.
○ Produce a warning when stock levels drop below a pre-set restock level.

Designing the file / record structure

We will be using a random access file structure. This will allow us to update the stock levels. Because we are using a random access system, we will have to use fixed length fields. We therefore need to work out just how much space we are going to need for each record. There will be just six records – one for each type of chocolate, and each record will consists of three fields:

○ The chocolate type will need to be stored as a string. We need to work out the maximum string length we are going to use. Once this is set up it cannot easily be changed, so we need to consider the longest possible case. In this case, is **Cherry Supreme** which is 14 characters long.
○ Both the current stock level and the restock level can be stored as integers. VB uses 2 bytes to store integers. This means each record will need 18 bytes of memory space.

Process design

Figure 8.1 shows how the solution will work. There will be one main menu form that will have links to all the other forms.

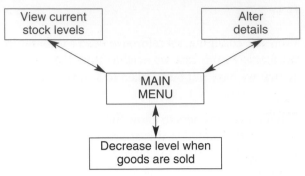

Figure 8.1

It is important to think through how each of the processes listed above will work.

Alter stored details

A potential problem with projects like this is how to enter the data into the system in the first place. We can get round this by using the update process to enter details of the first record.

○ The data will be displayed on screen in three control arrays – one each for type, restock level and current level.
○ Clicking a **SAVE** button will allow all details to be stored. There needs to be an **Are you sure?** button to allow the user to confirm the update.

View current stock levels

○ Details of each type, stock and restock level will automatically load when the form is first opened.

Alter stock levels as goods are sold or new stock is made.

○ Display all six types along with their current stock level.
○ Include a third column where the user can enter details of goods sold.
○ Use a command button to subtract the goods sold from the stock level, then save the details to file.

Low stock level warning

This process needs to be carried out whenever the stock levels are changed. Alice's Chocolates has asked that this happens automatically, so the user should not need to ask if any stock needs replenishing. The logical place for this to happen is therefore after every change to stock level.

○ Compare each current stock level with the reorder stock level and warn accordingly.

Designing the user interface

Figure 8.2 shows the layout of the form used to alter any of the stored details. Note that control arrays have been used to store the details of the type, current and restock levels.

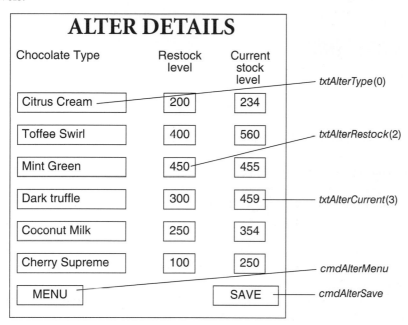

Figure 8.2

The forms for viewing current stock levels and updating when stock has been sold will follow a similar format.

Working with random access files

Before we can start on the forms we need to set up the random access file structures. We do this by creating a **user-defined variable**.

VB supports three types of variables:

○ Local variables that are only available within a specific procedure. These are defined within the procedure itself.
○ Global variables that are available within a given form. These are defined at the start of the code for a form.
○ Global variables that are available across a whole project. These must be declared in a separate module.

The user-defined variable needs to be available across the whole project, so we need to set up a module for it to be stored in.

1   Open VB and save a blank project to a new folder.

2   Select **Add Module** from the Project menu.

Figure 8.3

3   Click on **Open**. A blank code screen called **Module1** will appear.

4   Add the following lines of code to the module:

```
Type RecordDetails
  RecordType As String * 14
  RecordCurrent As Integer
  RecordRestock As Integer
End Type
```

Data normally consists of just one item. For example, it might be a string, a real or a date. However, it is possible for a data type to be made up of a number of other data types. This code creates a data type that stores all the data for one record. Our user-defined data type is going to be called **RecordDetails**. It will have three parts.

This routine declares the data type `RecordType` as a string. The `* 14` on the end tells VB that the maximum length that will be allowed is 14 characters. The other two components are both going to be stored as integers. They take up 2 bytes each so each record will be 18 bytes long.

5   Create a form called **frmMenu** like the one shown in Figure 8.4.

6   Use suitable names to identify the three command buttons.

Figure 8.4

The maximise and minimise buttons have been removed by changing the **BorderStyle** property of the form to **1-Fixed Single**.

7   Create a second form called **frmAlterRecords**. The design for this form is shown in Figure 8.2 and Figure 8.5 shows one possible solution. Note that you will not be entering text in the controls at this stage – we will be doing this later.

Alice's Chocolates

ALTER DETAILS

Type	Restock level	Current stock
Citrus Cream	200	234
Toffee Swirl	400	560
Mint Green	150	167
Dark Truffle	300	459
Coconut Milk	250	354
Cherry Supreme	100	250

MENU   SAVE

Figure 8.5

8   Create code that links the **Menu** and **Alter Records** forms.

The code attached to the **MENU** button on **frmAlterRecords** form will look like this:

```
Private Sub cmdAlterMenu_Click()
  frmAlterRecords.Hide
  frmMenu.Show
End Sub
```

Create similar code to link the menu to **frmAlterRecords**.

Now we can set up the **SAVE** routine.

9   Load up the code design page for **frmAlterRecords** and move to the top of the page.

10 Add the following line:

```
Private SaveRecord As RecordDetails
```

This line declares a variable called `SaveRecord` which will use the user-defined data type `RecordDetails` we set up earlier.

11 Double-click on the **SAVE** button in **frmAlterRecords**, and VB will create the following procedure:

```
Private Sub cmdAlterSave_Click()
End Sub
```

12 Add the following code to the procedure.

```
Open "ChocFile.txt" For Random As #1 Len = 18
For RecordCount = 1 To 6
SaveRecord.RecordType = txtAlterType(RecordCount - 1)
SaveRecord.RecordCurrent = _
Val(txtAlterCurrent(RecordCount - 1))
SaveRecord.RecordRestock = _
Val(txtAlterRestock(RecordCount - 1))
Put 1, RecordCount, SaveRecord
Next
Close #1
```

The line `Open "ChocFile.txt" For Random As #1 Len = 18` tells the computer to open a random access file called **ChocFile.txt**. If no file of this name can be found, a new file will automatically be created.

The **txt** extension on the file name is only there to help us. It means we can load the file directly into a text editor so we can check to see what the file contains. `Random` tells the computer this will be a random access file, which means it can be accessed for both reading and writing. Finally, the `len = 18` tells the computer how long each record is going to be.

We now need to take the details for each chocolate type in turn and save them to the file as a record. This is a repetitive process, so we will use an iterative routine – a **For/Next** loop. There are six records to save so the loop runs from RecordCount is 1 to 6.

The next three lines take the details from the appropriate elements of the control arrays and puts them in the variable `SaveRecord`. There is an anomaly that needs explaining here. Although the records that are stored in the file are numbered 1 to 6, the elements of the control arrays are numbered from 0 to 5. This is why each of the three lines that loads the control array elements into `SaveRecord` ends with − 1.

`Put 1, RecordCount, SaveRecord` is the line that does the actual saving for us. It takes the contents of `SaveRecord` and saves it to a specific record in the random access file. The position it saves to is determined by the variable `RecordCount`. The 1 tells the computer to send this data to the file currently attached to file identifier 1.

13 Run the program and enter the data supplied by the user to set up records for the six types of chocolate. When you have finished, you might want to open the file **ChocFile.txt** to make sure it has all worked.

Once you are happy you have set up the data in the file, there is one final step. This procedure is designed to show the latest settings, but if you exit the program then rerun it and enter the **Alter** routine, the text boxes will be empty. This is because we have not told the computer to load them from the file.

14 Double-click on the **Alter Records** form, double click in the form and add the following code to the `Form_Load` procedure:

```
Open "ChocFile.txt" For Random As #1 Len = 18
For RecordCount = 1 To 6
Get 1, RecordCount, SaveRecord
txtAlterType(RecordCount - 1) = SaveRecord.RecordType
txtAlterCurrent(RecordCount - 1) = _
SaveRecord.RecordCurrent
txtAlterRestock(RecordCount - 1) = _
SaveRecord.RecordRestock
Next
Close #1
```

This is almost the exact mirror image of the lines we looked at earlier on.

`Get 1, RecordCount, SaveRecord` accesses the random access file connected via file identifier 1 (in this case **ChocFile.txt**), goes to record number `RecordCount` and reads the record it finds there into the variable `SaveRecord`.

There are two final problems to resolve.

Refreshing the form

The form **AlterRecords** now seems to do all we expected of it, but the problem is that the form is only refreshed when it is opened for the first time. This is because the procedure `Form_Load` is only carried out when a form is first opened. The solution is to close the form properly.

15 Find this line of code in the procedure `cmdAlterMenu_Click`:

```
frmAlterRecords.Hide
```

and change it to:

```
Unload frmAlterRecords
```

This will force VB to shut down this form, so when you next ask to view it, it must be completely reloaded, which includes a complete refresh of the contents.

The other problem is that the specification calls for some sort of verification check before the data is saved.

Adding a message box

16 Find the procedure `cmdAlterSave_Click` and add the following lines directly after the procedure is defined:

```
ErrorType = MsgBox("Are you sure you want to save?", _
vbYesNo + vbDefaultButton2, "WARNING")
If ErrorType = 7 Then
Exit Sub
End If
```

When you save new details the following message box will be displayed (see Figure 8.6).

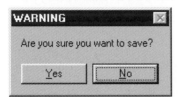

Figure 8.6

A message box has three parts – what appears as the message, some sort of numerical information that tells the message box what to display and how to react to a mouse click, and the text that appears in the title bar. The text in this message box is self-explanatory, but the numbers are much less obvious.

○ `vbYesNo` and `vbDefaultButton2` are **systems constants** which means that they translate directly into numbers. `vbYesNo` equals 4 and `vbDefaultButton2` is 256 so you could have put 4 + 256 instead of these names. Using systems constants, like these, makes programs easier to follow.

○ `vbYesNo` makes the message box display a **Yes** and a **No** button. `vbDefaultButton2` makes the **No** button the default. This forces the user to select the **Yes** key rather than just pressing return.

Once either the **Yes** or **No** button has been pressed, the message box returns a value. In this case, the value has been called `ErrorType`. If **Yes** is pressed then `ErrorType` is set to **6**, and if **No** is pressed then `ErrorType` becomes 7.

The **If/Then** shown below then makes use of this value to decide whether or not the save procedure should be carried out:

```
If ErrorType = 7 Then
Exit Sub
End If
```

If the user selects **No** the variable ErrorType is set to 7 and the procedure is exited using the Exit Sub command.

17 Test your code by running the program.

Adding code to view the records

18 Create the form **frmViewRecords** like the one shown in Figure 8.7. Note that the columns of text controls are elements of three control arrays.

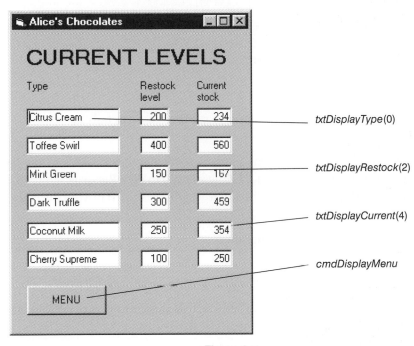

Figure 8.7

This data will need to be loaded from the file every time the form is loaded. This will be achieved by making use of the **Form_Load** procedure.

19 Create a link between the **VIEW STOCK LEVELS** button on **frmMenu** and this new form.

The link from **frmViewRecords** back to **frmMenu** needs to use the **Unload frmViewRecords** rather than **frmViewRecords.Hide** so that the form will be refreshed every time it is reloaded.

20 Once again we will be using the user-defined variable type **RecordDetails** so you need to add the following line to the top of the code attached to the form **frmViewRecords**:

```
Private DisplayRecord As RecordDetails
```

21 Double-click on the form and add the following code to the resulting `Form_Load` procedure:

```
Open "ChocFile.txt" For Random As #1 Len = 18
For Counter = 1 To 6
Get 1, Counter, DisplayRecord
TxtDisplayType (Counter - 1) = _
DisplayRecord.RecordType
TxtDisplayCurrent (Counter - 1) = _
DisplayRecord.RecordCurrent
TxtDisplayRestock (Counter - 1) = _
DisplayRecord.RecordRestock
Next
Close #1
```

This is exactly the same code that was used to load the record details in
`frmAlterRecords`.

You could argue that these two forms are almost identical – they both show the same
information — but there is one important difference: **frmViewRecords** is a **read only**
form — it has no save procedures attached to it — whereas the **frmAlterRecords**
allows the user to do just that.

22 Test your code by running the program.

Adding code to alter the stock levels

23 Create the form **frmUpdateRecords** like the one shown in Figure 8.8. Note that
the columns of text controls are elements of five control arrays.

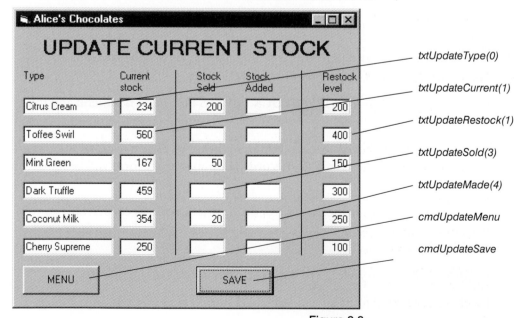

Figure 8.8

This form looks similar to the previous two, but it has two extra columns where the user can enter details of how many chocolates have been sold and/or added to the existing stock.

24 Add code that links this form with the **MENU** form. Again, you will need to use the **Unload** method.

25 Set the **Enabled** property of the control arrays used to store the type, current and restock levels to **FALSE**. This will stop the user trying to alter these values.

26 Add the following line to the start of the code view of **frmUpdateRecords** so that we can use the user-defined record type:

```
Dim UpdateRecord as RecordDetails
```

We need to make sure that the details of the current stock level are loaded from the file into the form.

27 Create a `Form_Load` procedure and add the following lines of code to it.

```
Open "ChocFile.txt" For Random As #1 Len = 18
For Counter = 1 To 6
Get 1, Counter, UpdateRecord
txtUpDateType(Counter - 1) = UpdateRecord.RecordType
txtUpDateCurrent(Counter - 1) = _
UpdateRecord.RecordCurrent
txtUpDateRestock(Counter - 1) = _
UpdateRecord.RecordRestock
Next
Close #1
```

28 Double-click on the **SAVE** button and add a message box that will make sure the user really wants to update the records. Remember to use the `Exit Sub` command if the user decides not to save.

29 Add the following lines of code, which will update the stored details

```
Open "ChocFile.txt" For Random As #1 Len = 18

For RecordCount = 1 To 6
txtUpDateCurrent(RecordCount - 1) = _
Val(txtUpDateCurrent(RecordCount - 1)) + _
Val(txtUpdateMade(RecordCount - 1)) - _
Val(txtUpDateSold(RecordCount - 1))
txtUpDateSold(RecordCount - 1) = ""
txtUpdateMade(RecordCount - 1) = ""
Next
```

```
For RecordCount = 1 To 6
UpdateRecord.RecordType = txtUpDateType(RecordCount - 1)
UpdateRecord.RecordCurrent = _
Val(txtUpDateCurrent(RecordCount - 1))
UpdateRecord.RecordRestock = _
Val(txtUpDateRestock(RecordCount - 1))
Put 1, RecordCount, UpdateRecord
Next

Close #1
```

There are two main parts to this procedure.

The first part updates the values that are held on screen. The **For/Next** loop takes each row of data in turn, adds the number of chocolates that have been added to the stock and subtracts those that have been sold. The program then resets the values held in the **Stock Sold** and **Stock Added** columns to blank.

The second part of the code should be very familiar to you by now. It takes the contents of the control arrays and saves them to the file.

Adding code to check the restock levels

The fourth and final task in this project is to check to see if the company needs to make any more chocolates to bring the stock levels back up.

We need to carry out this check immediately after any update.

30 Add the following lines to the end of the procedure `cmdUpdateSave_Click`:

```
ErrorMessage = ""
For RecordCount = 1 To 6
If Val(txtUpdateCurrent(RecordCount - 1)) < _
Val(txtUpdateRestock(RecordCount - 1)) Then
ErrorMessage = ErrorMessage + _
txtUpdateType(RecordCount - 1) + vbCrLf
End If
Next

If ErrorMessage <> "" Then
MsgBox "You need to restock the following chocolates" _
+ vbCrLf + ErrorMessage, vbCritical, "WARNING"
End If
```

The first section of this routine works as follows:

○ The variable `ErrorMessage` is going to act as a store – it will record all the types of chocolate that need restocking but it starts as empty.

- ○ We have used a **For/Next** loop to repeat the process of checking each type of chocolate in turn.
- ○ The **If/Then** selection inside this loop checks to see if a particular type needs restocking. If it does, then the name of the type of chocolate is added to `ErrorMessage`. The `vbCrLf` forces the next name to be added on the next line.

The second part of this routine checks to see if `ErrorMessage` is empty. The `<>` signs mean **does not equal**, so if `ErrorMessage` does not equal nothing (a sort of double negative) then the message box is called up (see Figure 8.9).

Figure 8.9

Note how the `vbCritical` brings up a different icon on the message box.

Controlling the focus by setting tab stops

Even though your screen may be full of frames and controls, only one of them is actually in use at any one moment in time – this frame or control is said to have the **focus**.

Most users know you can use the tab button on the keyboard to move from one control to the next. You can control the route the tab key takes your user around a form. This might also include missing out controls that you do not want them to have access to.

For example, although the update form in this task consists of thirty text boxes and two command buttons, we are really only interested in entering data into twelve text boxes and using the two command buttons.

Each control has two properties related to tab stops — **TabIndex** and **TabStop**.

The **TabIndex** property controls the order in which the controls are visited. Once a form has gained the **focus** the control with the **TabIndex = 0** is given the focus within the control. Pressing the TAB key will move the focus on to the control that has **TabIndex = 1** and so on.

TabStop indicates whether a control is part of the tab list. If this property is set to FALSE then it is missed out.

31 Change the **TabIndex** and **TabStop** properties of your forms to help the user enter data as efficiently as possible.

32 Test your code by running the program.

⊕ Unit 9 Project Seven (I) – Chris' Car Customiser

Task   Chris owns a small workshop where he customises cars. Customers take him their cars and, as long as the car is capable of being converted, he will do the job. He used to do a rough estimate of how much a job was going to cost but, as his customers are asking for more and more features, he is finding it increasingly difficult to work out an accurate price.

Chris has asked you to set up a computer system that will do the following:

- ○ Allow Chris and the customer to decide what options are going to be fitted. Obviously they want to be able to review the list and change features as they go along.
- ○ The system needs to give a price for the job. This quote will be valid for 30 days, after which the customer will have to be re-quoted.
- ○ Chris wants to be able to print out the quote so both he and the customer have a permanent record of what they have agreed.

This table shows the prices Chris currently charges:

WINDOWS	
No change	–
All Electric	450
Front Electric	250

SUNROOF	
No change	–
Manual	300
Electric	560

PAINT	
No change	–
Pearl	600
Metallic	720
Colours	
Fierce Red	
Quick Silver*	
Sunset Blue	
Ink Black**	

EXTRAS	
Alloy wheels	280
Sat. Navigation	320
Leather seats	200
Heated seats	100
Surround sound	60
Tinted glass	240
Tow bar	180
Fluffy dice	5

*Quick Silver is not available in pearl paint

**Ink Black is not available in metallic paint

Aim   To introduce frames, option buttons and check boxes.

Specification

○ The solution must be easy to use, and it must clearly indicate to the customer which features have been agreed on.

○ We only need to create one form for this job. This will need text boxes for the customer's name and address. We also need to store details of the car that is to be converted. These are probably going to include the car's make, model and registration.

○ Because the quote is only good for 30 days, we need to show the date the quote was made.

○ We will use a combination of check and option boxes so the customer can pick the features they want.

○ Individual prices and the overall cost might well be a deciding factor, so this needs to be updated immediately.

○ There won't be room on the screen for the command buttons we have used in previous tasks, so we will be using a menu bar instead.

○ We need to be able to print out a quote, so the customer has a record of what has been decided.

○ We need to be able to store the details. We could use either a serial or a random access file structure, but we will actually be storing each quote in its own file. These files will be stored in a folder called Car Quotes.

○ Chris needs to be able to load a quote back up so that he and his customers can review it.

○ Quotes that are out of date will need to be deleted.

This project is going to involve a lot of work, so for convenience the sections about printing and saving the details to file will be dealt with in the next unit.

Designing the user interface

Load	Save	Print	Clear

Name		Windows	Sunroof

Name

Address

Car Reg

Make/Model

Date

Windows
○ No change
● All electric
○ Front electric 450

Paint
○ No change
○ Pearl
● Metallic 720

○ Fierce Red
● Quick Silver
○ Sunset Blue
○ Ink Black

Sunroof
● No change
○ Manual
○ Electric 0

Extras
☐ Alloy wheels 0
☐ Sat. Navigation 0
☐ Leather seats 0
☐ Heated seats 0
☐ Surround sound 0
☐ Tinted glass 0
☐ Tow bar 0
☐ Fluffy dice 0

Total 1170

Figure 9.1

This design will take up most of the screen and there will be a lot of details in view. It would be a good idea to group similar information, placing the customer and car details in one area of the screen, with details of the work to be carried out in another.

1 Open VB and save the project into a new folder.

Working with frames

We are going to put each section of this form into its own frame. There are two reasons for this. First, the frame will help to keep the component parts together visually. The second reason is that the frame will tell VB which option buttons belong together.

2 Click on the [xy] **Frame** icon on the Toolbox and drag out a frame for the **Customer Details** (see Figure 9.2).

3 Use the **Caption** property of the frame to change the name to **Customer**.

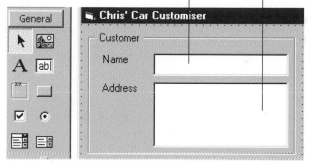

4 Add labels and suitably named text controls for the customer's name and address inside this frame (see Figure 9.2). Set the Address text box to Multiline.

5 Create two more frames for the car's details and for the date (see Figure 9.6).

Figure 9.2

6 Add the appropriate text boxes into the two new frames. Call the text controls **txtCarReg** and **txtCarMake**.

7 Double-click on the form and in the resulting `Form_Load` procedure set the date text box to automatically set to today's date when the code is executed. See page 55 if you have forgotten how to do this.

8 Add a new frame to show the **Windows** options as shown in Figure 9.3.

Adding option buttons

9 Click on the [⊙] **Option button** icon in the Toolbox and add an option button to the **Windows** frame.

10 Name this button **optWindow**.

11 Copy and paste so that you have three copies of the option button. We are going to use a control array so click on **YES** when prompted. It is vital that you copy and paste within the frame or the option buttons will not work correctly.

12 Change the **Caption** property of each to those shown in Figure 9.3.

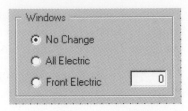

Option buttons are also known as radio buttons. The idea is that you can only select one of the options at a time.

Figure 9.3

We need to set one of the buttons to be the default. You do this by changing the **Value** property of one of the controls to **True**.

13 Set the **Value** property of the **No Change** button to **True**.

14 Add a text box that will eventually show the cost of the windows. This control should be named **txtCostWindow**.

15 Set the **Text** property to **0** and align it to the right.

16 Use this same process to set up a frame for the **Sunroof** options shown in Figure 9.6, name the option control **optSunroof**. Call the textbox **txtCostSunroof**.

You might have noticed by now that if you drag a frame then everything that you have placed in the frame moves with it.

The **Paint** options will be made of two frames, one inside the other. The main frame will be used to show the paint type and the other, inside frame, will display the colours.

17 Set up a **Paint** frame and set up option buttons for **No change**, **Pearl** and **Metallic**. Name the option control **optPaintType**. Call the text box **txtCostPaint**.

18 Make the **No Change** button the default setting. You will need to make sure that there is enough space at the bottom of this frame for the colour options.

19 Add a new frame inside the **Paint** frame, and add the four colour options name this **optPaintColour**. Again, these should be elements of a control array. Make **Fierce Red** the default option and add a text box for the cost.

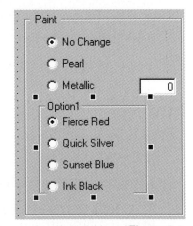

20 Now set the option frame's **BorderStyle** property **0–None**.

Figure 9.4

This will make the border disappear so the colour buttons now seem to be part of the **Paint** frame. We really need to set the colours so that they cannot be selected unless they are available with the selected type. We will be looking at how to **grey out** later.

Adding check boxes

21 Add a new **Extras** frame as shown in Figure 9.6.

22 Click on the ☑ **CheckBox** icon and add a check box to the **Extras** frame.

23 Rename the control **chkExtra**.

We are going to use a control array for the check box control.

24 Copy and paste the control you have just set up until you have eight check boxes.

25 Change the **Caption** property for each to match the details given in Figure 9.6.

Like the option buttons we set up earlier, the value property of a check box indicates the current state of the button but, unlike the option buttons, a check box can be either **0**, **1** or **2**. A value of **0** indicates it is **unchecked** and **1** that it has been **checked**. A value of **2** shows the checkbox is **greyed out**.

26 Add a text box control array that will eventually store the cost of the extras that have been selected. This array should be called **txtCostExtra**.

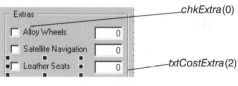

Figure 9.5

27 Finally, add a text box control that will eventually store the cost of the quote of the job. Ideally this should be placed in its own frame. Name the text box **txtQuote**.

Figure 9.6

Adding the code

We now need to go back and make all the buttons and boxes we have set up work.

28　Double-click on one of the **optWindow** controls to create a procedure called
`optWindow_Click`. Add code to the procedure so that it looks like this:

```
Private Sub optWindow_Click(Index As Integer)
   Select Case Index
   Case 0: txtCostWindow = "00"
   Case 1: txtCostWindow = "450"
   Case 2: txtCostWindow = "250"
   End Select
End Sub
```

Using a control array makes this code very straightforward. When the program is running,
a click on any of the **optWindow** buttons will call up this procedure. The value of `Index`
in the opening line indicates which element of the control array has been clicked.

The `Select Case` statement takes this value and compares it with 0, 1 and finally
2. When it finds a match it changes the window's cost box accordingly. So clicking on
the **All Electric** option sets `Index` to be 1 and the `Select Case` construct finds a
match and puts the value 450 in the cost box.

29　Add similar code to make the **Sunroof** and **Paint** cost boxes work. The values are:

```
No change = 0
Manual = 300
Electric = 560
Pearl = 600
Metallic = 720
```

There is an additional problem with the paint selection process. If the **No Change**
button is selected you should not be able to choose a colour. If the **Pearl** button is
selected we want every button apart from the **Quick Silver** option to be enabled, and
the **Metallic** button should leave every colour apart from **Ink Black** available.

30　Find the `optPaintType_Click` procedure and add the following lines after
the second `Case` selection line as shown:

```
Case 1: txtCostPaint = "600"
  optPaintColour(0).Enabled = True
  optPaintColour(1).Enabled = False
  optPaintColour(2).Enabled = True
  optPaintColour(3).Enabled = True
Case 2: txtCostPaint = "720"
```

31　Execute the program and click on the **Pearl** paint option.

You will notice that the colour buttons now look like Figure 9.7. Setting the **Enabled** property to false has disabled (or greyed out) the option.

32 Add suitable code to make all the colours turn off when you click on **No Change** and all but the **Ink Black** turn on when you click on the **Metallic** button.

33 Because the default in this frame is **No Change** you need to set the enabled property of each of the four colours to **False** at the design stage so they will not show up when the program is first executed.

Figure 9.7

There are just two more problems we need to resolve with this frame. You cannot have a car painted in **Pearl Quick Silver**. But if you have chosen this colour then go back and change the paint type to **Pearl** the program will currently accept the change. We need to ensure this does not happen.

34 Add the following code immediately after the `Case` 1 line in the procedure `optPaintType_Click`:

```
Case 1: txtCostPaint = "600"
If optPaintColour(1).Value = True Then
MsgBox"Pearl paint is not available in Quick _
Silver.", 16, "WARNING"
optPaintColour(1).Value = False
End If
```

This selection checks to see if paint colour element 1 (the **Quick Silver** button) is currently selected. If it is, a message box is displayed and the **Quick Silver** button has its value set to **0** so it is no longer the selected colour (see Figure 9.8).

Figure 9.8

35 Add similar code to make sure you cannot select a car with **Ink Black Metallic** paint.

Working with check boxes

We are now going to deal with the **Extras** frame.

36 Double-click on the first extra, which should be **Alloy Wheels** and the procedure `chkExtra_Click(Index As Integer)` will appear in the code view. Add the following code to the procedure:

```
If chkExtra(0).Value = 0 Then
txtCostExtra(0) = "0"
Else
txtCostExtra(0) = "280"
End If
```

37 Execute the program and click on **Alloy Wheels**. The price will toggle between **0** and **280**.

Because each of the values that appear in the extra cost text boxes are different, there is no simple way of coping with the other seven extras the customer might select. If we copy and paste the code you have just entered, this procedure will have 40 lines of code. This is going to make it unwieldy. We will therefore use a different technique. We will set all the text boxes back to the default value of **0** then look at each check box in turn and if it has a value of **1**, we will change the matching cost box accordingly.

38 Delete the code inside this procedure and enter the following code instead:

```
For Counter = 0 To 7
  txtCostExtra(Counter) = 0
Next
If chkExtra(0).Value = 1 Then txtCostExtra(0) = "280"
If chkExtra(1).Value = 1 Then txtCostExtra(1) = "120"
If chkExtra(2).Value = 1 Then txtCostExtra(2) = "200"
If chkExtra(3).Value = 1 Then txtCostExtra(3) = "100"
If chkExtra(4).Value = 1 Then txtCostExtra(4) = "60"
If chkExtra(5).Value = 1 Then txtCostExtra(5) = "240"
If chkExtra(6).Value = 1 Then txtCostExtra(6) = "180"
If chkExtra(7).Value = 1 Then txtCostExtra(7) = "5"
```

Adding code to calculate the cost

Every time there is a change to the details that the user wants, the total cost needs to be recalculated. This will ensure that the quote that is being displayed will always be up to date.

39 Go to the end of the code and add in the following new procedure. You will have to type in the whole thing because this is a user-defined procedure – one we are setting up ourselves:

```
Private Sub AddUp()
txtQuote = Val(txtCostWindow) + Val(txtCostSunroof) + _
Val(txtCostPaint)
For Counter = 0 To 7
txtQuote = Val(txtQuote) + Val(txtCostExtra(Counter))
Next
End Sub
```

For now we will ignore how we get this procedure to work, and concentrate on what it does.

It works by adding together the sub-totals in the **Window**, **Sunroof** and **Paint** frames and storing the result in the text control **txtQuote**. It then uses a **For/Next** loop to work down the list of eight elements in the `txtCostExtra` array.

By the time the procedure has finished, the control **txtQuote** will contain all the values added together.

Now we need to tell the computer when to carry this procedure out. This needs doing at the end of each of the four procedures we have already set up. For example, the procedure for calculating the cost of the windows will now look like this:

```
Private Sub optWindow_Click(Index As Integer)
  Select Case Index
    Case 0: txtCostWindow = "0"
    Case 1: txtCostWindow = "250"
    Case 2: txtCostWindow = "450"
  End Select
  Call AddUp
End Sub
```

The `Call` informs VB that this is a request to carry out the procedure called `AddUp`. It then carries out the user-defined procedure you have just created and puts the latest total in the **txtQuote** control.

40 Add the `Call AddUp` line to all the necessary procedures.

41 Now run the program and fill in some details to check that the program works.

The details for the final tasks that involve printing and saving the details can be found in the following unit.

⊕ Unit 10 Project Seven (II) – Chris's Car Customiser

In Unit 9 we set up a user interface that allowed Chris and his customers to create a quote for customising a customer's car.

The tasks that are still to be completed are:

○ Save quotes so they can be recalled and possibly amended at a later date.
○ Print out a quote for the customer to take away with them.
○ Find all the quotes that have gone beyond their 30 day limit.

Aim   To introduce the menu bar. Using common dialog boxes.

Creating menu buttons

Figure 10.1 shows the user interface with **File** and **Print** menu options.

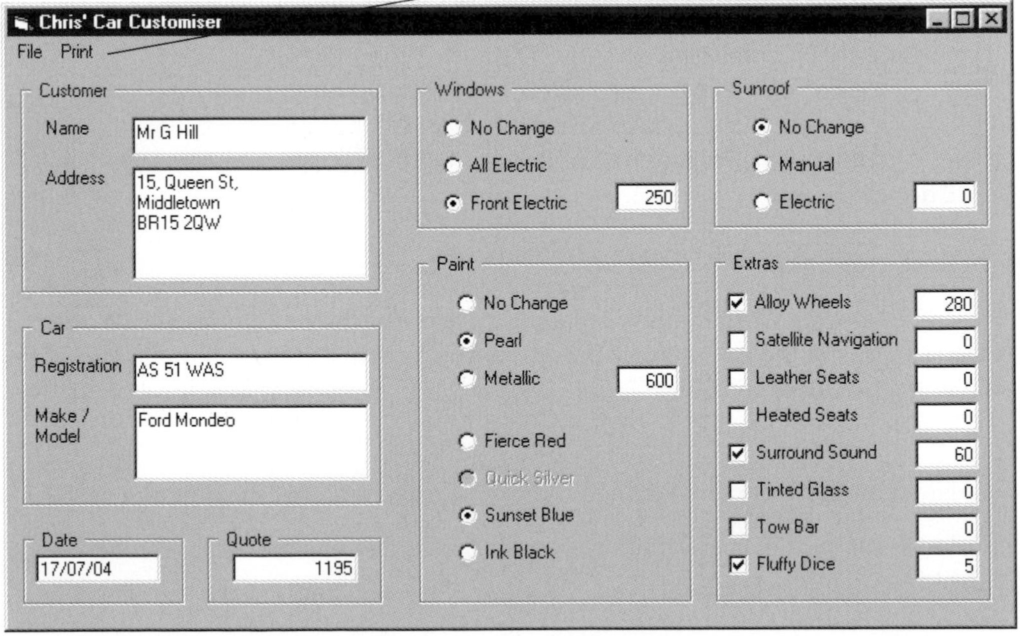

Figure 10.1

Previous projects have used command buttons to carry out tasks such as printing text boxes and navigating between forms. Command buttons undoubtedly have their uses, but they also take up valuable space on a form and they are not as versatile as drop-down menus. They can also look rather cumbersome.

We are going to use menu buttons to control how the computer works with files and a printer.

1   Open the design view of the form by selecting **Menu Editor** from the **Tools** menu.

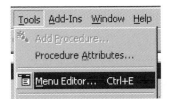

Figure 10.2

This will open the **Menu Editor** window:

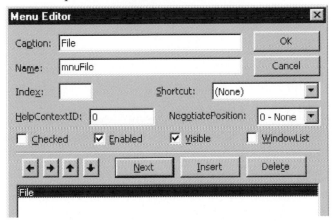

Figure 10.3

2   Enter **File** in the **Caption** box, and **mnuFile** in the **Name** box, as shown in Figure 10.3, then click on **Next**.

When the user selects the **File** menu when the program is runnng, we want a drop-down menu to appear showing **Load** and **Save** like that shown in Figure 10.5.

3   Click on the **→** button on the menu control page.

This tells VB to set up a sub-menu. A row of dots will appear below **File** in the display window.

4   Enter **Load** and **mnuLoad** in the **caption** and **name** boxes and click **Next** again.

5   Create a **Save** option for the menu bar and name this option **mnuSave**. Click Next.

VB assumes this will be part of the same menu.

We now need to add **Print** to the list but it will not be part of the **File** sub-menu.

6   Click on the button then add **Print** and **mnuPrint**.

Figure 10.4

7   Close down the menu edtior by clicking **OK**.

You will now find that your form has two menu items and, if you click on **File**, a drop-down menu appears (see Figure 10.5).

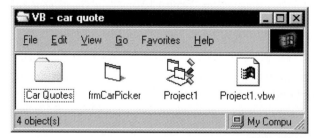

Figure 10.5

Saving records to a file

Each quote will be saved as a file in a folder. We will be using the car's registration number as the file name. This is convenient because each registration number, and therefore the file name is unique. However, we need to do some preliminary work before we can use this method.

8   Find the folder that contains the components of this project and add a folder called **Car Quotes**.

Figure 10.6

9   Add the following line of code to the start of the `Form_Load` procedure:

```
ThisDir = CurDir + "\Car Quotes\"
```

The computer keeps track of whereabouts you are in the directory structure by using a system variable called **CurDir**. This stores the current directory (or folder). This line of code takes this value and adds the rest of the path name for the folder you have just created. We will need to use the variable **ThisDir** in more than one procedure, so we need to declare it as a public (or global) variable.

10 Go right to the start of your code and add the following code as the first line:

```
Public ThisDir As String
```

11 Click on on the **Save** menu option. This will create a new procedure called `mnuSave_Click()`.

12 Add the following line of code to the procedure:

```
Open (ThisDir + txtCarReg + ".cqu") For Output As #1
```

This will open a new file in the **Car Quotes** folder. It will add a **cqu** file extension. **cqu** is short for **car quote**. The computer will not recognise this file type, but it will not complain about it either. We will be using this file extension later in the program.

13 Now we can save the details of the quote to the file. Add the following code to the procedure:

```
Print #1, txtDate
Print #1, txtCustName
Print #1, txtCustAddress
Print #1, "AddressEnd"
Print #1, txtCarReg
Print #1, txtCarMake
For Counter = 0 To 2
If optWindow(Counter) = True Then Print #1, Counter
Next
For Counter = 0 To 2
If optSunroof(Counter) = True Then Print #1, Counter
Next
For Counter = 0 To 2
If optPaintType(Counter) = True Then Print #1, Counter
Next
For Counter = 0 To 3
If optPaintColour(Counter) = True Then Print #1, _
Counter
Next
For Counter = 0 To 7
Print #1, chkExtra(Counter)
Next
Close #1
```

You may have chosen to use slightly different control names in your form, but the names you have used will be very similar to these.

The data about the customer and their car is saved as a series of `Print #1`, statements – a technique we used in Unit 6. Note the `AddressEnd`. We will be looking at this later in this unit.

There are then four very similar **For/Next** loops. Each option button group has only one button that is currently selected, and the value property of that control is set to **True**. Each **For/Next** loop checks this **Value** and saves the number of the element of the array that is currently selected. This might look cumbersome, and there are other methods we could have used to save the data, but as you will see below, this method of saving the data makes recreating the quote very easy.

The fifth and final **For/Next** loop works in a very different way. Only one button can be selected in a set of option buttons, but any number of boxes can be selected in a group of check boxes. The fifth **For/Next** loop saves the value of each of the eight elements of the control array `chkExtra`.

14 Run the program and enter and save a quote for a customer. Close the program then locate and open the file you have just created. It should look something like Figure 10.7. The file will be named using the car registration you type in and will be in the Car Quotes folder. It can be opened with Notepad.

```
20/07/04
Mr H Ford
45, Hill Street,
Middeltown
SD32 4EW
AddressEnd
AS 53 WAS
Vauxhall Vectra
1 ⎫
1 ⎬  These four values show the chosen options
1 ⎭  for each of the four option button groups.
2
0 ⎫
1 ⎪
0 ⎪
0 ⎬  These eight values signify whether or
1 ⎪  not a check box has been selected.
1 ⎪
0 ⎭
1
```

Figure 10.7

Loading files using a common dialog box

A lot of programs share a number of common features. For example, when you **Save As** or **Print** from most standard applications, you see a standard interface. These are examples of **Common Dialog Boxes**.

Common dialog boxes are not immediately available, so you have to tell VB that you want to use them.

15 Select **Components** from the **Project** menu.

16 Select the version of **Microsoft Common Dialog Control** that your copy of VB is using and click on the **OK** button.

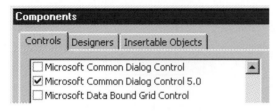

Figure 10.8

You will notice that a new icon has been added to the Toolbox (see Figure 10.9).

17 Click on this 🔲 **Common Dialog** icon and place a copy anywhere you like on the form.

The icon will not show when the program is executed, so it does not matter where you place it on the form.

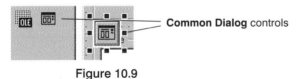

Common Dialog controls

Figure 10.9

Like all other controls, common dialog boxes have properties.

18 Change the name of this control to **cdlFile**.

19 From the interface design window select **Load** from the File menu. A new procedure will appear:

```
Private Sub mnuLoad_Click()

End Sub
```

20 Add the following code to the procedure:

```
cdlFile.ShowOpen
```

21 Execute the program and try out the **Load** button. You will find you can navigate to the Car Quotes folder you created earlier. See Figure 10.10.

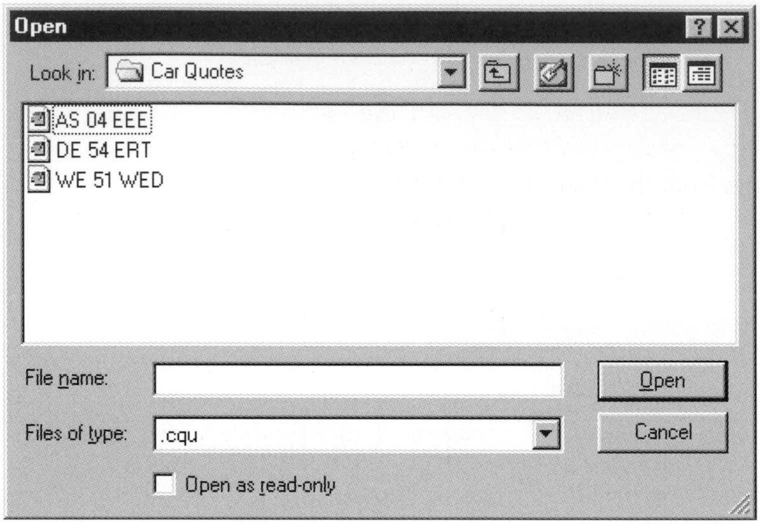

Figure 10.10

Common dialog boxes can be used to open a number of common windows, so the new line tells VB to use it as an **Open** window.

Once the **Open** window is open, the user must click on either **Open** or **Cancel** to exit the window. In order to make the computer recognise when the **Cancel** button has been clicked, we have to make it believe this is an error.

22 Open the **Properties** window for the dialog box and change the **CancelError** property to **True**.

Now the program will generate an error when **Cancel** is pressed so we need to make use of this.

23 Amend the procedure so it looks like this:

```
Private Sub mnuLoad_Click()
    On Error GoTo TrapError
    cdlFile.ShowOpen
    Exit Sub
    TrapError:
End Sub
```

The `On Error GoTo TrapError` line forces the computer to go to the line `TrapError:` if an error occurs anywhere in the procedure. The `Exit Sub` makes the program exit the procedure before it gets to the error trapping section.

Reading the details from the file

We now need to read the data from the file and put it back into the form so that the quote is recreated.

24 Add the following lines after the line `cdlFile.ShowOpen`:

```
Open cdlFile.filename For Input As #1
Line Input #1, Temp: txtDate = Temp
Line Input #1, Temp: txtCustName = Temp
Line Input #1, Temp: txtCustAddress = Temp
Close #1
```

25 Execute the program and load one of the files you have saved.

You will notice that there is something wrong with the address; only the first line has been loaded from the file. This is because VB uses carriage returns, commas and various other symbols to determine where a line or field ends. This is why we have included the text field **AddressEnd**. We are now going to use this to load the entire address.

26 Delete the line:

```
Line Input #1, Temp: txtCustAddress = Temp
```

and replace it with:

```
txtCustAddress = ""
Temp = ""
Do
  If Temp <> "" then txtCustAddress = _
        txtCustAddress + Temp + vbCrLf
  Line Input #1, Temp
Loop Until Temp = "AddressEnd"
```

This iterative process keeps on reading lines from the **cqu** file until it comes across the line **AddressEnd**. This value has been used as a flag to indicate the end of the address.

Now we must load the features the owner wanted.

27 Run the program again and load a file. The complete address should now load.

28 Add the following lines to the existing code directly after the code above.

```
Input #1, Temp: txtCarReg = temp
Input #1, Temp: txtCarMake = Temp
Input #1, TempOpt: optWindow(TempOpt).Value = True
Input #1, TempOpt: optSunroof(TempOpt).Value = True
Input #1, TempOpt: optPaintType(TempOpt).Value = True
Input #1, TempOpt: optPaintColour(TempOpt).Value = True
```

```
For Counter = 0 To 7
Input #1, TempOpt: chkExtra(Counter) = TempOpt
Next
```

Notice how, in these and the other input lines of code, the data is read from the file and placed in a temporary variable called **Temp** or **TempOpt**. This has to be done because you cannot read data directly from a file into a VB control. We have had to use two different variables for this because there are two sorts of data — text and numeric.

Run the program to check that it displays all the correct data in the form.

Printing using a common dialog box

There are several methods we can use for printing. We could print the form as it appears on the screen, but this does not look very good on paper. It would be much better if we could control what appears on the paper and where, so another option would be to create a new form that had all the details set out exactly where you wanted them and then print out that form instead. You might want to try this method to see how easy it is to do.

The third option is to use VB to control the layout of the output document. This is the method we will be using.

29 Add another **common dialog control** to your form and name it **cdlPrint**.

30 Set the **CancelError** property of this new control to **True**.

31 From the design window, click on **Print**. The following procedure will be created:

```
Private Sub mnuPrint_Click()

End Sub
```

You need to add the error trapping. If you do not, the printer will attempt to print irrespective of which button you press.

32 Add the following lines of code to the procedure:

```
On Error GoTo traperror
CdlPrint.ShowPrinter
Exit Sub
traperror:
```

33 Add the following lines of code after `cdlPrint.ShowPrinter`:

```
Printer.FontName = "Times New Roman"
Printer.FontBold = True
Printer.FontSize = 18
Printer.Print "Chris's Car Quotation"
Printer.EndDoc
```

The command word `Printer` supports a wide variety of parameters, and it would be a good idea if you experimented to find the layout that suits you best. The last line – `Printer.EndDoc` – forces the printer to print out the page regardless of how much will actually appear on it.

Once you have set a property, it will remain in force until you change it. So, unless you change the font details everything else you print on the page will be in Times New Roman bold in font size 18.

34 Add the following lines before the `Printer.EndDoc` command.

```
Printer.Print
Printer.FontName = "Courier New"
Printer.FontBold = False
Printer.FontSize = 12
Printer.Print "Date            "; txtDate
Printer.Print "Name            "; txtCustName
Printer.Print "Car reg         "; txtCarReg
Printer.Print "Car type        "; txtCarMake
```

The first of these lines, `Printer.Print`, forces a gap in the printed output and the following three lines change the font details.

Courier New is a mono-spaced font and its use will help with the overall layout. Note how spaces have been used to line up the data.

35 Add the following lines:

```
Printer.Print "Windows - ";
If optWindow(0).Value = True Then Printer.Print " no _
change ";
If optWindow(1).Value = True Then Printer.Print _
"front electric ";
If optWindow(2).Value = True Then Printer.Print " _
all electric ";
Printer.Print txtCostWindow
```

Adding a semicolon (;) to the end of a print statement forces the computer to stay on the same line so that a line such as:

```
Windows — all electric 450
```

will appear on the paper.

36 Add suitable code as above to show the chosen options for **Paint Type**, **Paint Colour** and **Sunroof**.

Finally, we need to print out the **Extras** the customer has asked for.

37 Add the following lines of code:

```
For Counter = 0 To 7
If chkExtra(Counter).Value = 1 Then
Printer.Print Left(chkExtra(Counter).Caption, 12);
Printer.Print Tab; txtCostExtra(Counter)
End If
Next
```

The loop looks at the value of each of the option boxes in turn and only prints out if it is set to **True**.

The `Left(chkExtra(Counter).Caption, 12)` forces VB to only print out the 12 left-most characters.

The `Tab` forces the costs into a new column.

38 Add suitable code to add the total cost of the quote.

Printing out details in this way is very labour intensive – you end up producing a lot of code and it can take quite a lot of time and effort to reach a suitable result.

39 Print out a quote to check your code works.

Chris's Car Quotation

```
Date           29/08/04
Name           Mrs E Wilde
Car reg        WE 51 WED
Car type       Ford Galaxy

Windows - no change          0
Paint Type - metallic       720
Paint colour - sunset blue
Sunroof - no change          0

Alloy Wheels   280
Leather Seat   200
Heated Seats   100
Surround Sou    60

Total          1360
```

Figure 10.11

Adding code to find out-of-date quotes

The final process is to check through each of the quotes that have been stored and check to see if it is more than 30 days old.

The process will be:

○ Look at each file in a specified folder.
○ Check to see if it is the file type we are using — in this case **cqu**.
○ Load the file and check the date.
○ Query all dates that are more than 30 days ago.
○ Display the file and query for the deletion.
○ Delete files as necessary.

40 Add a suitable menu bar option for this process (see Figure 10.12) called mnuCheck.

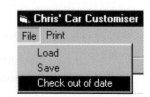

Figure 10.12

41   Click on the new menu option to create a new procedure:

```
Private Sub mnuCheck_Click()
End Sub
```

We now need to make the program read through the list of files in the folder and read in and check the date of each one.

42   Add the following code to the procedure:

```
CheckFile = Dir(ThisDir, vbNormal)
Do While CheckFile <> ""
   CheckFile = Dir
Loop
```

If you look back, you will find we set up the variable `ThisDir` to store the pathname to the folder **Car Quotes**. This code tells the computer to create a variable called `CheckFile` which will initially hold the name of the first file it finds in that folder.

The program then checks to see if the file name is blank. If it is then there are no more files to check.

The line `CheckFile = Dir` changes the value of the variable to the next filename in the folder. The `Loop` finishes the iteration process started with the `Do While` line.

43   At the moment, this code doesn't actually do anything useful, so add the following lines of code immediately after the Do While line:

```
If Right(CheckFile, 3) = "cqu" Then
End If
```

This selection process checks the rightmost three characters of the variable `CheckFile`, which is the file's extension. You will remember that we are using an extension of our own called **cqu**. If the file has this extension then we know it is one of ours, so now we need to open the file and read the date.

44   Dates can be awkward to work with, so VB has a special **Date** format. Add the following line to the start of this procedure:

```
Dim TempDate As Date
```

This declares a local variable called `TempDate`.

45   Add the following code inside the `If/End If` selection process:

```
Open CurDir + "\Car Quotes\" + CheckFile For Input As #1
Line Input #1, TempDate
If Date - TempDate > 30 Then
txtDate = TempDate

End If
```

The variable `CheckFile` holds the name of the next file in the folder **Car Quotes**, so this line opens the next file ready for the data to be read from it.

The first item we stored in the file was the date. This algorithm loads this data from the file then subtracts it from `Date`. This is the system variable used by VB to show today's date. If the result is greater than 30 then the quote is more than 30 days old, so we need to display all the details of the quote.

46 We have already created code to read and display a file's contents. Find the procedure `mnuLoad_Click()` and copy and paste the relevant code. The first line of code you need is:

```
Line Input #1, temp: txtCustName = temp
```

and the last four are:

```
For Counter = 0 To 7
Input #1, TempOpt: chkExtra(Counter) = TempOpt
Next
Close #1
```

47 Make sure you copy **all** the code between and including these lines.

This code will display all the files that the program finds, one after the other, but we need to be able to view each one and decide if we want to keep or delete the file.

48 Add the following code:

```
ErrorType = MsgBox("This quote is more than 30 days _
old." + vbCrLf + "Do you want to delete it?", vbYesNo _
+ vbDefaultButton2, "Check Quote")
If ErrorType = 6 Then
    Kill ThisDir + CheckFile
End If
```

We came across message boxes in a previous unit. This algorithm uses two more systems variables – **vbYesNo** and **vbDefaultButton2**. **vbYesNo** adds **Yes** and **No** buttons to the message box and **vbDeaultButton2** makes the second button (the **No** button) the default button. This means that the user will have to select **Yes** if they want to delete the file.

The command `Kill` does just that — it kills or deletes a file. You need to be very careful how you use it — there is no 'Are you sure?' safety net, so you may wish to add another message box to provide the user with a double check.

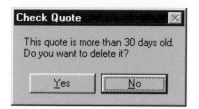

Check Quote

This quote is more than 30 days old.
Do you want to delete it?

Yes   No

Figure 10.13

There is one final step. If the quote is not more than 30 days old then the details will
not be taken from the file and, more importantly, the file will not be closed down.

49 Add the following lines immediately after `Kill ThisDir + CheckFile`:

```
End If
Else
Close #1
```

This may look rather messy, but it is merely the tidying stage of a whole sequence of
nested constructs.

⊕ Unit 11 Project Eight – The Fruit Selector

Task   You have been asked by a primary school teacher to design a program that will help pupils in Year 1 (age 5/6) to learn the names of fruit and associate them with the correct picture. The teacher has already decided how she wants the program to work. She wants the computer to pick an image at random from a selection of about ten. This picture will be displayed along with the names of four fruit, one of which is the right match for the picture. The pupils are then expected to click on the matching word and a message will be displayed so that they know if they have chosen correctly. An error message will be displayed if they choose the wrong name.

Aim   Working with graphics, timers and random numbers.

Designing a solution

○ The program will be used by five and six year olds, so we have to presume that they only have limited language skills.
○ It would be a good idea if the teacher could add and delete pictures in the 'bank', so that she can introduce new fruit in order to keep using the program through the year, or possibly even use pictures of another topic, such as transport.

We need to sort out the processes needed, the user interface and how we will store the images.

The human compute interface (HCI) must be really simple, both to look at and to use.

Although we could make the program start displaying images as soon as it is executed, it will probably be better to have a **Start** button. This will be in the centre of the form but it will need to disappear once it has been pressed.

Images will be stored in a folder called **ImageFolder**. They will all need to be stored as bitmap images. The file names will be used as the names on the screen, so the image in Figure 11.1 will be called **Banana.bmp**, but the text in at least one of the text boxes will be **Banana**.

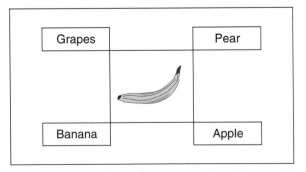

Figure 11.1

As soon as the program is executed, the program will need to access the folder of images, count the number of images and load the names into an array.

Once the **Start** button has been pressed, the program needs to do the following:

○ Pick an image at random from a list.
○ Load and display the image.
○ Show the name of the fruit in one of the four surrounding boxes. This location also needs to be a random selection.
○ Select three other fruit names at random and display them in the remaining three boxes. This might lead to the same name appearing more than once.
○ The user will click on the name that they think matches the image.

The system will then:

○ Check to see if the name in the box matches that of the fruit.
○ Display a tick of some sort for a short time, then restart if the pupil selects the correct name.
○ Display some sort of simple error message, then restart, if the pupil selects the wrong name.

At present there is no plan to show a score of how many fruits the pupil correctly identifies. This would need recording, but it is doubtful if the children using the program would be able to make any use of the information, although it might be useful for the teacher.

Creating the form

1 Create a new folder for the project.

2 Add a folder inside your project folder called **ImageFolder** and put a number of bitmap images in the folder. The names of the image files will be used in the screen display. See Figure 11.2.

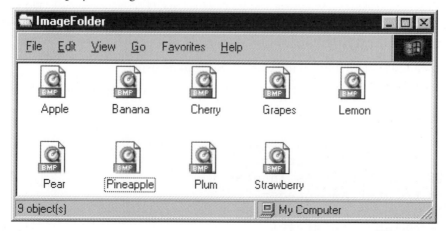

Figure 11.2

3 Open a new VB project and save it to the appropriate folder.

4 Set up the form and add an **Image** control to the centre of the form and set its **Stretch** property to **True**. This will mean the size of the control will not change. Call this control **imgDisplay**. VB also has a Picture Box control, so be careful to use the Image Control.

5 Add four text controls around the image. These need to be four elements of a control array and they will be elements **0**, **1**, **2** and **3**. It doesn't matter how you arrange them, but the array should be called **txtShowName**. You might want to centre the text and increase the font size.

6 Finally add a command button called **cmdStart** to the centre of the image (see Figure 11.3).

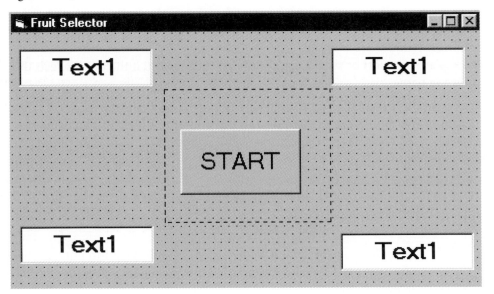

Figure 11.3

Declaring the variables

First we need to declare the variables we are going to be using.

7 Open the code window and add the following lines to the blank page:

```
Option Explicit

Dim ImageName() As String
Dim CheckFile As String
Dim ChosenFruit As Integer
Dim Counter As Integer
Dim ImageCounter As Integer
Dim ThisDir As String
```

These are the variables we will be using:

○ The array `ImageName` will store the names of the files in **ImageFolder**, but, as we don't know how many of them there are, we cannot dimension the array yet. We will have to re-dimension it later, which is why there is no number between the brackets.
○ `CheckFile` will be used to store the names of the files as they are read from the folder.
○ `ChosenFruit` will record the number of the image file that we will be displaying.
○ `Counter` is going to be used as a general-purpose counter in **For/Next** loops.
○ `ImageCounter` will record how many images there are in the folder.
○ `ThisDir` will store the pathname that points to the folder the program is stored in.

Getting started

Now we need to load details of the folder **ImageFolder**. This needs doing before the user makes their first selection, so it will be carried out in the `Form_Load` procedure.

8 Open the `Form_Load` procedure by double-clicking on the form, **not** a control, and add the following code to it:

```
Randomize
ThisDir = CurDir
```

We will be using VB's built in random number generator to pick the images. Unless we tell the computer to **randomize**, we will always get exactly the same sequence of seemingly random numbers. We will be looking at how you can generate random numbers later in this unit.

The line `ThisDir = CurDir` stores the pathname for the folder that contains `ImageFolder`.

We now need to find how many image files there are in the folder. This number will be stored in the variable `ImageCounter`.

9 Add the following code to the `Form_Load` procedure:

```
ImageCounter = 0
CheckFile = Dir(ThisDir + "\ImageFolder\", _
vbDirectory)
Do While CheckFile <> ""
 If LCase(Right(CheckFile, 3)) = "bmp" Then
 ImageCounter = ImageCounter + 1
 End If
CheckFile = Dir
Loop
```

We came across this process in the previous unit. The algorithm reads in the file names one at a time. `ImageCounter` is increased by one each time a new file name is read in. The selection process ensures that only files with a **bmp** extension are counted. It does this by looking at the three right-most characters. `Lcase` ensures they are all lower case letters.

10 Add the following code to the procedure:

```
ReDim ImageName(ImageCounter)

Counter = 0
CheckFile = Dir(ThisDir + "\ImageFolder\", _
vbDirectory)
Do While CheckFile <> ""
 If LCase(Right(CheckFile, 3)) = "bmp" Then
 Counter = Counter + 1
 ImageName(Counter) = Left(CheckFile, Len(CheckFile) - 4)
 End If
 CheckFile = Dir
Loop
```

This code re-dimensions the array that will store the file names. It then reads the names into the array ImageName.

When we declared the variables earlier we created an array called `ImageName`, but we didn't state the number of elements the array would have. Now we know, we can set the `ReDim` command.

The line:

```
ImageName(Counter) = Left(CheckFile, Len(CheckFile) - 4)
```

removes the file extension from the filename. We need to do this because we will be using the filenames in the HCI. The code in this line uses the function `Left`. This function takes the left-most characters from a string. In this case it takes the length of the string (using the function `Len`) and subtracts 4 from it. This removes the file extension and the **.** from the file name.

Working with random numbers

Next we will sort out what happens when the user clicks on the **Start** button.

11 Double-click on your **Start** button and add the following code to the procedure you just created:

```
ChosenFruit = Int(ImageCounter * Rnd()) + 1
imgDisplay.Picture = LoadPicture(ThisDir + _
"\ImageFolder\" + ImageName(ChosenFruit) + ".bmp")
```

`ImageCounter` is being used to store the number of images in the image file, so we need to pick a whole number between 1 and `ImageCounter`. VB has a **random number generator**, but unfortunately there is no simple way of making it produce a whole number in the range we want. For now you should imagine that there are 9 images in the folder so the variable `ImageCounter` will be **9**.

The function `Rnd()` returns a random number between 0 and 1. It can be 0, but it cannot actually be 1. Multiplying this by `ImageCounter` returns a value between 0 and **8.999**. The function `Int` truncates a number. This means it removes any decimal part, so taking the `Int` of the value we have leaves a whole number between 0 and 8. Finally we add 1 to produce a random number between 1 and 9.

The second line uses this value and the list of file names we stored earlier to create the pathname to one of the files in the image folder.

The command `LoadPicture` does what it says – it loads a graphic into the image control **imgDisplay**.

Run your program and click start. The images should load in the image box. A different image will load each time you press the Start button.

Now we need to add four random names to the four text boxes – we will make sure one of the names matches the fruit a little later.

12 Add the following code to the **cmdStart** procedure:

```
For Counter = 0 To 3
txtShowName(Counter) = ImageName(Int(ImageCounter * _
Rnd()) + 1)
Next
```

This uses the same technique to make up a random number between 1 and `ImageCounter`. This random number is then used to select one of the file names from the array `ImageName`. The loop repeats this process four times – once for each of the four elements in the text box control array.

Next we need to make sure that the right name for the fruit appears in at least one of the text boxes. We have just put names in each of the four text boxes and it is possible that none of them is the right one. The algorithm in the next line will overwrite one of them with the correct answer.

13 Add the following single line to the procedure:

```
txtShowName(Int(4 * Rnd())) = ImageName(ChosenFruit)
```

This line picks a random number between 0 and 3 and puts the name of the fruit that is being displayed in that text box.

14   Finally, hide the **Command** button by adding the following line of code:

```
cmdStart.Visible = False
```

15   Save and run the code you have now created.

One of the images you saved to the **ImageFolder** earlier on will now appear in the centre of the form and it should be surrounded by four fruit names including the name of the fruit itself.

Tidying up the user interface

16   Close the program.

Now we need to decide how to respond when the user clicks on one of the four text boxes.

If the pupil selects the correct name then a tick will appear in the image control you have already set up. If they choose the wrong name, then a message will appear on the screen telling them what the right fruit name was.

17   Add a label control to the form. Call the control **lblWrong**. Figure 11.4 shows this on the bottom of the form. Make the label 'disappear' by setting the caption property to be empty.

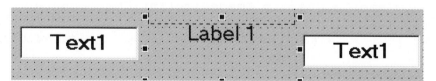

Figure 11.4

18   Find a suitable **Tick** symbol (see Figure 11.5) and store it in your main folder as **Tick.bmp**.

Figure 11.5

19   Click on any one of the four text boxes and the following procedure will be created. Change its name to **txtShowName_Click**.

```
Private Sub txtShowName_Click(Index As Integer)
End Sub
```

This procedure uses a parameter to indicate which of the four text boxes has been clicked. This data is held in the variable `Index`. Note that `Index` will therefore be a number between 0 and 3.

20 Add the following code to the procedure:

```
If txtShowName(Index) = ImageName(ChosenFruit) Then
imgDisplay.Picture = LoadPicture("tick.bmp")
Else
lblWrong.Caption = "The answer was " + _
ImageName(ChosenFruit)
End If
```

This selection process compares `txtShowName(Index)`, which is the name that is stored in the text box that has been clicked on, with `ImageName(ChosenFruit)`, which is the name of the chosen fruit. If they are the same then the tick is loaded into the image control. If they are not the same then the text in the label is set up to show what the correct answer is.

21 Test the code you have written so far.

The code seems to work, but in fact it only ever produces one fruit to choose then it seems to stop working. This is because we have not yet told the computer that we want to repeat the process all over again.

Before we can repeat the selection process we need to make the program pause for a short while, otherwise the tick and/or error message will never be seen.

Using a timer

We need to add a timer to the program.

22 Click on the **Timer icon** on the Toolbox and place it anywhere on the form – it doesn't matter where it goes because it will not show up when the program is executed.

23 Rename the timer control **Timer**. Set the **Enabled** property to **False** and the **Interval** property to **1500**. This number determines how long the program will pause for. Once you have got the program as you want it, you might try different values in here.

24 Add the following single line of code to the end of the `txtShowName_Click` procedure:

```
Timer.Enabled = True
```

This means the timer control is now active.

25 Double-click on the timer control you have just created and the following procedure will be created:

```
Private Sub Timer_Timer()
End Sub
```

The procedure you have just created is unusual in that it does not need user intervention for it to be accessed. Once the timer control has been **enabled**, the control is visited regularly. The frequency with which it is visited depends on the **Interval** property. This is measured in milliseconds, so the value of **1500** you entered earlier means it will be visited every 1.5 seconds.

26 Add the following code to the timer procedure:

```
Timer.Enabled = False
lblWrong = ""
cmdStart_Click
```

The first line disables the timer so that the timer procedure will not be visited again until a `Timer.Enabled = True` command is executed.

The second line sets the caption in the label to be nothing, so it effectively disappears. The final line calls the procedure `cmdStart_Click`. This is the procedure we created earlier that selects a new fruit and puts four fruit names in the four text controls.

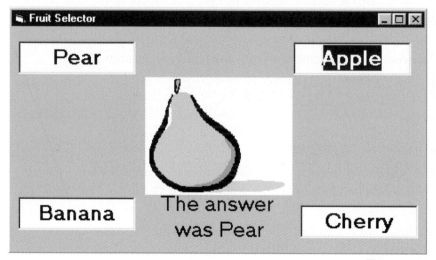

Figure 11.7

Extension tasks

1 At present this program goes on forever, or at least until the user shuts it down. Add suitable code to make the program select 10 fruit pictures then display a score out of 10.

2 Add code that allows the user to create a bank of sets of images for the pupils to choose from.

⊕ Unit 12 Project Nine – The video hire shop

Task A relational database has been set up to store details of the customers and videos in a Video Hire shop. The owner wants to be able to search for his customers by name from within the customer form.

Aim Introduce VBA in Access. Use VBA to search.

Introduction to VBA

VBA is short for Visual Basic for Applications and is a version of VB that is embedded in a lot of Microsoft's products. Being able to use VB inside application packages such as Excel or Access gives you much more power and flexibility when you are dealing with your data.

In this case, the user interface has already been created for you, and the screenshots below show how the database has been put together. It is assumed that you have a working knowledge of Access and that you can create a basic relational database.

▦ Customer Management	_ □ ✕
▸ Customer ID	5
Customer ForeName	Helen
Customer Surname	Hudson
Customer DoB	06/11/76
Record: ⏮ ◀ 5 ▶ ⏭ ▶* of 12	

Figure 12.1

This form has been set up using standard Access features.

We need to add a search facility that will let the user search by name and then display the matches it finds. We will also be adding a control that will show how many matches have been found.

VBA is very similar to VB – it supports the same controls and uses the same language concepts, but as you will see there are also some features that are specific to VBA.

1 Create and save an Access database to store the customer details.

2 Use the attribute names shown in Figure 12.1.

3   Set Customer ID as AutoNumber, ForeName and SurName as Text and DOB as Date.

4   Add some customers to the form as test data.

Adding command buttons

We are now going to add a text box and command button to the **Customer** form that will allow us to enter a search name and then search for it.

5   Open the **Customer** form in **design** view.

6   Click on the maximise button to make the form bigger so there is room for these controls.

7   If the toolbox is not visible, right-click on the form and select **Toolbox**.

8   Use the toolbox to add **ab|** **Text box** control. Note that the text box control looks different in VBA compared to VB.

9   Add a command button but cancel the **Command Button Wizard** form when it appears.

You will notice that creating a text box has also set up a label and that each control is numbered sequentially. In Figure 12.2, the label has been called **Text8**, the text box **Text9** and the command button **Command10**.

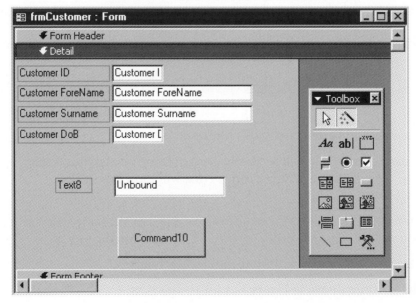

Figure 12.2

As in our other VB work, we need to rename these controls.

10 Right-click on the command button and select **Properties**.

The resulting table allows you to alter the caption property via the **Format** tab and the name property via the **Other** tab.

11 Change the control name to **cmdSearch** and the caption to SEARCH.

Alternatively, you can change both the **Name** and **Caption** properties under the **All** tab.

12 Change the name of the text box to **txtFindName**. You might also want to change the caption of the label.

Adding code to command buttons

Now we can add the code that will search for whatever you enter in the text box.

13 Right-click on the command button and select **Build Event...** then **Code Builder**, then click **OK**.

Figure 12.3

You will now see some more typically VB features, including the code view and the tools that let you access the properties.

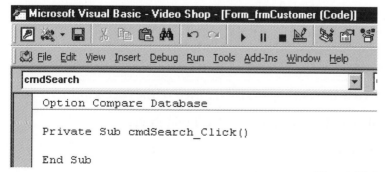

Figure 12.4

Programming with Visual Basic

We are going to carry out the search on the customer's forename.

14 Add the following code to the resulting **cmdSearch_Click** procedure:

```
Customer_ForeName.SetFocus
DoCmd.FindRecord "Mary"
```

The first line tells VBA which particular attribute in the record to search. The name of the attribute that we are using to store the forename is actually called **Customer Forename** with a space between the two words. VBA cannot cope with spaces so we need to use an underscore to replace the space.

15 Test the code by closing the code editor and switching to **Form View**.

You will notice that clicking on the **Start** icon does not allow you to test the code. It has to be run by clicking the command button on the form.

Note that if you have not got a customer with the forename **Mary** in your customer table then the search will stay on whichever record was already being displayed.

The **DoCmd** command is very powerful and it has many methods that can be used with it.

The **FindRecord** command does just that – it finds the first record that matches the criteria. The **FindRecord** command is followed by up to seven parameters.

The example searches through all the records for an exact match for the word **Mary**. This is not case specific so **mary** would also be matched.

Full details of all the parameters can be found in Appendix 4 or in the built-in help routines in VBA.

Adding code to carry out a search

This is only a very simple search and there are a number of refinements we need to make to make it useful, including the following:

o Search using data from a text box.
o What to do if there are no matches.
o What to do if there is more than one match.

16 Go back to the VBA code by selecting the Design view of the Access form.

17 Right-click on the SEARCH command and select Build Event.

18 Change the DoCmd line to:

```
DoCmd.FindRecord txtFindName
```

19 Exit the code view and open the Access form in **Form view**.

20 Enter a name in the **txtFindName** text box that you know is in your database and click on **Search**.

Your program should now be showing the first record that has a matching name.

What to do when no matches are found

21 Enter a name you know is **not** in your customer table and try to search for it.

There is no indication that the code has failed to find a match – the current record is still being displayed.

22 Enter the following code after the DoCmd line:

```
If Customer_ForeName <> txtFindName Then
  MsgBox "Failed to find any matching records.", _
0, "Search Failed"
  txtFindName.SetFocus
  Exit Sub
End If
```

This code compares the forename that is currently being displayed with the value you are searching for. If they are not the same then the search has failed to find any matches and a message box displays a suitable message.

The line txtFindName.SetFocus ensures that once the user has clicked on **OK** in the message box, the cursor returns to the text box ready for the user to try another name.

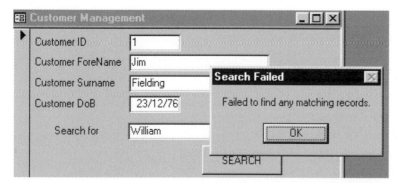

Figure 12.5

23 Clear the text box and click on **SEARCH** again. The following error message will be generated.

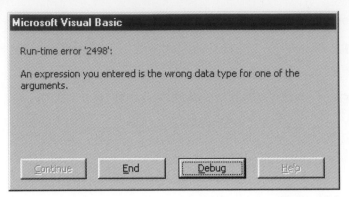

Figure 12.6

This error has occurred because VBA has nothing to search for. In fact the text box **txtFindName** contains a **null** value so we must use the `IsNull` function to check for this.

24 Add the following code at the start of the procedure:

```
If IsNull(txtFindName) = True Then
  MsgBox "There is nothing to search for.", 0, _
"Search Failed"
  Exit Sub
End If
```

Adding code to count the number of records founds

Now we will build a counter and that will show how many matches have been found.

25 Open the form in Design view.

26 Add another text control and call it **txtMatchCount**.

27 Change the label that has also been created to show what the text control will be used for.

28 Open the code view for the **Search** command button.

29 Add the following code to the end of the procedure between EndIf and EndSub.

```
CountFind = 0
Do
  CurrentCustomer_ID = Customer_ID
  DoCmd.FindRecord txtFindName, , , , , False
  CountFind = CountFind + 1
Loop Until CurrentCustomer_ID = Customer_ID

  txtMatchCount = CountFind
```

The variable `CountFind` will keep track of how many matching records have been found.

The command `DoCmd.FindRecord txtFindName,,,,,,False` finds the next matching record in the table. Each time it does this the variable `CountFind` is incremented by 1. This is all placed inside a loop that finishes when the last matching record has been found.

In order to see if we have reached the last record we need to record the **CustomerID** of the record currently being displayed. Next we ask VBA to find the next record then look to see if `Customer_ID` has changed. If it hasn't then we have reached the last record.

Once the loop has been exited we can display the number of records in the text control you created earlier. Test your code.

⊞ Customer Management	☐ □ ✕
Customer ID	5
Customer ForeName	Peter
Customer Surname	Jubb
Customer DoB	06/04/78
Search for	Peter
Matches	3 SEARCH

Figure 12.7

Stepping through the found records

The final step is to allow the customer to view each of the matching records. In order to do this we need to add two cursor keys that will allow us to move forward and backward through the matches.

We will deal with the 'previous record' problem first.

30 Open the Access form in Design mode.

31 Use the Toolbox to create a new command button.

32 Choose the **Record Navigation** and **Goto Previous Record** options.

33 Select a suitable icon, then click on **Next**.

34 Change the control name to **cmdPreviousMatch**.

35 Select **Finish**.

36 Right-click on the resulting command button and select **Build Event....**

You will find that Access has already created code for us. The line `DoCmd.GoToRecord , , acPrevious` looks like it might be of use, but all it will do is to move on to the next record in the database irrespective of whether or not it matches our criteria.

37 Delete all the code inside the procedure.

38 Add the following code to the procedure so that it now looks like this:

```
Private Sub cmdPreviousMatch_Click()
  Customer_ForeName.SetFocus
  DoCmd.FindRecord txtFindName, , , acUp, , , False
End Sub
```

This uses the same technique we came across earlier, but you will notice that the fourth parameter has been set to `acUp` which forces VBA to look for previous matching records. Test your code.

39 Add a suitable **Next** command button.

Figure 12.8

40 Call this command button **cmdNextMatch**.

41 Create code to allow the user to move to the **Next Record**. It is the same code as with the previous match command except `acUp` should be changed to `acDown`.

There are two remaining problems. If you click on the **Previous** or **Next** button after a successful search, the program moves through the matching records until it reaches the first or last match then it just keeps reloading this match. Clicking on either the **Previous** or **Next** buttons after an unsuccessful search will generate an error message. We could remove both of these problems if we only allowed the **Previous** or **Next** command buttons to be visible if there is anything to move to.

42 Set the **Enabled** property of both the **Previous** and **Next** controls to **No**.

43 Replace the last line before the EndSub inside the `cmdSearch` procedure with:

```
ThisMatch = CountFind
txtMatchCount = ThisMatch & " / " & CountFind
If CountFind > 1 Then cmdPreviousMatch.Enabled = True
```

We are going to use the variable `ThisMatch` to keep track of which particular matching record is currently being displayed. The way we have set up the procedure means that the record that starts out being displayed is the last match.

The second line changes the display that appears on the form so that it now shows not only how many matches have been found, but also which particular record is currently showing.

If more than one matching record has been found we need to be able to move back through the matching records. The third line allows the **Previous Record** command button to be used.

Before we can make use of this algorithm we need to add two variable declarations to the start of the code.

44 Alter the start of the code so that it looks like this:

```
Option Compare Database
Dim CountFind As Integer
Dim ThisMatch As Integer
```

Now we can sort out what to do if the user clicks on the **Previous** button.

45 Alter the procedure `cmdPreviousMatch` so that it looks like this:

```
Private Sub cmdPreviousMatch_Click()
  Customer_ForeName.SetFocus
  DoCmd.FindRecord txtFindName , , , acUp , , , False
  cmdNextMatch.Enabled = True
  ThisMatch = ThisMatch - 1
  If ThisMatch = 1 Then cmdPreviousMatch. _
  Enabled = False
  txtMatchCount = ThisMatch & " / " & CountFind
End Sub
```

The four extra lines work as follows.

Having moved to the **Previous** record, we now need to be able to move back to the **Next** record so we set the **Enabled** property on the **Next** button to allow this.

This particular procedure deals with the clicks on the **Previous** button. We need to keep track of which record we are looking at, so we need to take one from the variable `ThisMatch`.

If `ThisMatch` is 1 then we are now at the first matching record. There is no point in allowing the user to try and move any further back, so we set the **Enabled** property to **False**.

Finally we change the display details so that the user can see which particular matching record they are looking at.

46   Change the procedure that copes with **Next** record button clicks to:

```
Private Sub cmdNextMatch_Click()
  Customer_ForeName.SetFocus
  DoCmd.FindRecord txtFindName, , , acDown, , , _
  False
  cmdPreviousMatch.Enabled = True
  ThisMatch = ThisMatch + 1
  If ThisMatch = CountFind Then _
  cmdNextMatch.Enabled = False
  txtMatchCount = ThisMatch & " / " & CountFind
End Sub
```

Extension tasks

1   If more than one matching record is found then the last record found is the one that is displayed first. Amend the code to show the first matching record.

 Unit 13 Project Ten – Alice's Chocolates stock control system

Task *Alice's Chocolates* has decided to use a database to help run their stock control. The details of each order are stored in a table called **Order**, stock details are kept in **Stock** and there is also a separate file called **Customer**.

Use VBA to create a system that subtracts a customer's order details from the stock file and issues any warning about low stocks.

Aim To extend the range of features used within VBA and Access.

Designing the solution

Set up an Access database in the normal way – details of the names to use are given below. As with the previous unit it is assumed that you have a good working knowledge of how to set up databases in Access.

We will set up an order form that will show all six chocolates that *Alice's Chocolates* sell. There will also be a check box that will indicate whether or not an order has been processed. There will be a command button which the user will click on to update the stock details. When the command button is pressed, the following processes will be carried out:

○ Check that the order has not already been processed.
○ Check each chocolate type to make sure there is sufficient stock to cover the order. If there is not, then produce a warning message but do not update the stock levels.
○ Update the stock levels.
○ Set the **order processed** check box to **Yes**.
○ Check to see if any chocolate types have gone below their reorder level.

Note: As there are only six items in the product range we will be listing the six within the order table rather than setting up a related stock table. Therefore the database is not fully normalised. Instead we will use VBA to link the amount ordered back to the stock table.

Setting up the database

1 Create a new Access database called **Alices Chocolates**.
2 Set up a table called **Stock** to store stock details.
3 Set the field names to **ChocType**, **CurrentStocklevel** and **Restocklevel**.

4 Set the field type for the first field to **Text**, and choose the **Number** field type for the remaining fields.

Since the names of the chocolates that Alice sells are never duplicated, you should also set the **chocType** field as the primary key for this table.

5 Create the records using the details in the table below.

CHOCOLATE TYPE	CURRENT STOCK LEVEL	INITIAL RESTOCK LEVEL
Citrus Cream	234	200
Toffee Swirl	560	400
Mint Green	455	450
Dark Truffle	459	300
Coconut Milk	354	250
Cherry Supreme	250	100

6 Create the **Customer** table and add fields for a customer ID and their name.

7 Make sure that the customer ID field is an **AutoNumber** and set as the primary key.

8 Add four records using made-up names for four customers.

9 Create an **Order** table.

10 The table should contain fields for an order ID, the customer's ID, the date and a field for each of the six chocolate types.

11 Add a field to show whether or not the order has been processed. This should be a Yes/No field named Order Processed. The default value of this should be set to **No**.

12 Use the record names and data types given in Figure 13.1

Field Name	Data Type
orderID	AutoNumber
custID	Number
Date	Date/Time
Citrus Cream	Number
Toffee Swirl	Number
Mint Green	Number
Dark Truffle	Number
Coconut Milk	Number
Cherry Supreme	Number
Order Processed	Yes/No

Figure 13.1

13 Create a one-to-many relationship between **Order** and **Customer**.

14 Create forms that can be used to control each of the three tables (see Figures 13.2, 13.3 and 13.4). Call these **frmCustomer**, **frmStock** and **frmOrder**.

Note that for the sake of clarity, no effort has been made to personalise these forms but you may choose to do so.

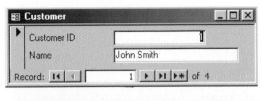

Figure 13.2

Figure 13.3

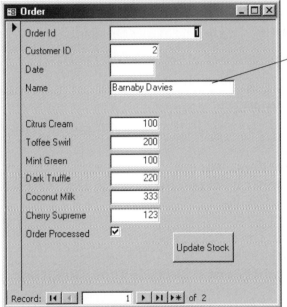

Note that CustomerName must be taken from the Customer Table. All other attributes are on the Order Table.

Figure 13.4

Adding the VBA code

15 Open the form **frmOrder** in Design view and, if it is not already open, open the Toolbox.

16 Add a command button to the form, but cancel the resulting wizard.

17 Change the caption to **Update Stock** and rename the control **cmdUpdate** by right-clicking the button and selecting **Properties**.

18 Right-click on the command button, then select **Build Event** then **Code Builder**.

You will now see the procedure associated with this control:

```
Private Sub cmdUpdate_Click()
End Sub
```

First we need to make sure that the order has not already been processed.

19 Add the following code to the procedure:

```
If [order processed] = True Then
MsgBox "This order has already been processed.", _
0, "WARNING"
Exit Sub
End If
```

The first line of code checks to see what value is currently being displayed in the text box [order processed]. The square brackets allow you to use controls with spaces in their names. The check box can be set to either **True** or **False**. We have come across message boxes in earlier units.

Now we need to check that there are enough of each of the chocolates that have been ordered to carry out this order.

20 Add the following lines to the procedure:

```
LowStock = ""
DoCmd.OpenForm "frmStock"
Forms!frmStock.Recordset.MoveLast
LastName = Forms!frmStock.ChocType
Forms!frmStock.Recordset.MoveFirst
  Do
    ThisName = Forms!frmStock.ChocType
    If Forms!frmOrder!(ThisName) > _
    Forms!frmStock![Current Stock level] Then LowStock _
    = LowStock + vbCrLf + ThisName
    Forms!frmStock.Recordset.MoveNext
  Loop Until ThisName = LastName
  DoCmd.Close

  If LowStock <> "" Then
    MsgBox "Unable to process order - stocks of the _
following" + vbCrLf + "chocolate(s) are too low to _
meet this order" + vbCrLf + vbCrLf + LowStock, 0, _
"WARNING"
    Exit Sub
  End If
```

Understanding the VBA code

There is a lot of code to decipher here, so we will work through it one section at a time.

```
LowStock = ""
DoCmd.OpenForm "frmStock"
Forms!frmStock.Recordset.MoveLast
LastName = Forms!frmstock.ChocType
Forms!frmStock.Recordset.MoveFirst
```

The variable `LowStock` will be used to record the names of all the chocolate types for which stock levels are too low to meet the order.

The second line opens the form `frmStock` so that we can access it and the underlying table.

We need to know what the name of the chocolate type in the last record in the file is so that we stop the program trying to move beyond the end of the file. The final line moves the file pointer to the first record in the form `frmStock`.

Notice the syntax of the code. The lines begin by identifying the type of object we want to look at – in this case `Forms`. The exclamation mark (`!`) indicates the next heading is contained inside this object. In this case it is the form `frmStock`. `RecordSet` indicates we want to work with the set of records, and the command `chocType` indicates the particular field we want to use within the record.

```
Do
ThisName = Forms!frmStock.ChocType
If Forms!frmOrder!(ThisName) > _
Forms!frmStock!Current Stock level Then LowStock = _
LowStock + vbCrLf + ThisName
Forms!frmStock.Recordset.MoveNext
Loop Until ThisName = LastName
```

The first line of code stores the chocolate type from the first record in the `frmStock` file in the variable `ThisName`. This should be **Cherry Supreme**. The program then looks for the value in the field with the line `Forms!frmOrder!(ThisName)`. In Figure 13.5 this is **300**.

Figure 13.5

The current stock level can be found by looking at the value of `Forms!frmStock!chocCurrent`. If the value held in the order is greater than the current stock level then the name of the chocolate is added to the variable `LowStock` with the code

```
LowStock = LowStock + vbCrLf + ThisName
```

The line:

```
Forms!frmStock.Recordset.MoveNext
```

moves the program on so that the next time it runs through the **Do/Loop** process, it will read the name of the next chocolate in the `frmStock` form so that this in turn is stored in the variable `ThisName`.

All through this process, the form `frmStock` has been open and, unless we do something about it, it will be left on the screen when we have finished the processing. The line `DoCmd.Close` closes the currently active form – in this case `frmStock`.

The final section of code looks to see if the variable **LowStock** is still empty. If it is not then at least one of the chocolate types must need restocking before the order can be processed. The statement `If LowStock <> ""  Then` checks for this. If it is not empty then an appropriate message box is displayed and the procedure is exited.

If the program moves beyond this then the order can be processed and we can subtract the details of the order from the existing stock.

21 Add the following code to the end of the procedure:

```
DoCmd.OpenForm "frmStock"
Forms!frmStock.Recordset.MoveFirst
Do
   ThisName = Forms!frmStock.Chocolate_Type
   Forms!frmStock!chocCurrent = _
Forms!frmStock!Current Stock Level - Forms!frmOrder! _
(ThisName)
   Forms!frmStock.Recordset.MoveNext
Loop Until ThisName = LastName

DoCmd.Close
```

The commands in this section of code are almost identical to the previous section. The code reopens the form `frmStock` and sets the pointer to the first record.

The only change is that instead of checking to see if there is enough stock, this code updates this value by reading in the existing stock level which is held in `Forms!frmStock!chocCurrent`. It then subtracts the value held in the appropriate text control on `frmOrder`.

Next we need to make sure that the order cannot be processed again by setting the value of the control **Order Processed** to **True**.

22 Add the following line of code:

```
Forms!frmOrder![order processed] = True
```

Finally, we need to check to see if any of the stock levels have now dropped below the reorder level.

23 Add the following code to the end of the procedure:

```
ReStock = ""
  DoCmd.OpenForm "frmStock"
  Forms!frmStock.Recordset.MoveFirst

  Do
     ThisName = Forms!frmStock.Choclate-Type
     If Forms!frmStock!Current Stock level < _
Forms!frmStock!ReStock level Then ReStock = ReStock _
+ vbCrLf + ThisName
     Forms!frmstock.Recordset.MoveNext
  Loop Until ThisName = LastName

  DoCmd.Close

  If ReStock <> "" Then
     MsgBox "The following chocolate(s) need re- _
stocking." + vbCrLf + vbrclf + ReStock, 0, "WARNING"
     Exit Sub
  End If
```

This uses the same routines as before. In this case, a variable called `ReStock` has been used to store details of the items that need restocking.

The other major difference is the line:

```
If Forms!frmStock!Current Stock level < _
Forms!frmStock!ReStock_Level Then ReStock = _
ReStock + vbCrLf + ThisName
```

This `If` statement checks to see if the value held in the `ReStock` field of the stock table is greater than the current stock level. If it is, then the name of the chocolate type is added to the variable `ReStock`.

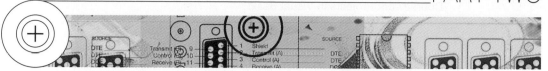

PART TWO

Coursework Projects in Visual Basic

⊕ Unit 14 Brief overview of the life cycle of a project

The life cycle describes the stages that you go through when creating a computer system and all of the associated documentation. It is referred to as a cycle because when you reach the final stage, you start all over again.

The definition used here is the one adopted by most exam boards and covers the main headings that are required for A2 coursework. This chapter is intended as an introduction to the contents of the life cycle and is also intended to give some general guidance on how to interpret it for A Level. Mark allocations quoted refer to the 2005/6 AQA Specification. Specifications change every year so you should check the current specification from your exam board.

It is common to show the life cycle as follows:

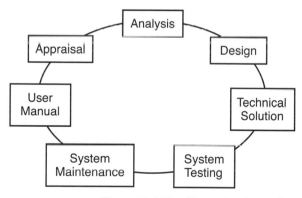

Figure14.1 The life cycle of a project

Analysis

Analysis is concerned with identifying and explaining the problem that you are trying to solve. It is critical that you find a real user with a real problem. A common mistake at this stage is to invent a problem that fits a solution rather than the other way round. For example, students may be experienced at handling files within VB and therefore contrive a project that involves this aspect.

Real users with real problems are essential and make your coursework easier to do. Much of the evidence needed for the analysis will come directly from the user. The alternative is that you have to make it up, which is harder to do and does not make for such a good project. For example, you will need to write sections on the background to the problem, who the person or organisation is that you are creating the system for and what they want to get out of it. If you have a real user, they will give you all of this information.

This analysis should lead to a realistic set of objectives by which you can judge the project later on. It is important to define the scope of the project. This means identifying what your new system will and won't do. It is a common mistake to take on a project that is either too easy or too hard. If your project is too easy then you will not be able to achieve the higher marks available in the mark scheme. If the project is too complex then you will spend all your time creating the solution and may lose marks in the write-up.

Design

Design involves all of the fine detail of specifying the solution to the problem. Although it is worth the same number of marks as the analysis, it is usually a much more detailed section. Many students are keen to rush ahead with the technical solution intending to come back to design later on. However, you should complete all aspects of the design first.

The only exception to this is that it may be the case that the solution will involve using parts of VB that you have not used before. This makes it very difficult to design 'on paper' as you don't know how you will solve it until you try. If this is the case, it would be worth writing pseudo-code or creating a prototype to allow you to generate the ideas for the design.

The importance of the design cannot be over-stated. Every year, a small percentage of students get half way through their projects and have to start again as they have not designed the system properly and they find that the solution they are using is not feasible.

Design covers every aspect of the creation of the solution, including defining the variables, writing sample code, defining file structures, designing the user interface and planning for testing. It is also helpful to create a number of diagrams including system flow charts or structure charts.

Technical Solution

This refers to the creation of the solution itself, in this case, a programmed solution to the problem written in VB. The exam board never request a live copy of your program. Instead, they require a printout of your code and they will give higher marks for code that is efficiently written and well-documented.

In terms of marks, the technical solution is worth around 23% of the total marks available for the coursework. The other 77% of the marks are for the write-up that goes with it. Inevitably, you will spend more than 23% of your total time programming the solution. However, as your project progresses and time becomes tight, you should bear in mind that your time will best be spent on the documentation rather than tweaking your code.

System testing

Testing means checking that your system works and that it does what it is supposed to do. You are likely to test your program as it progresses. It is common practice to write a section of code and then test it to ensure that it works. This is a good idea, but it is not enough on its own. There are four reasons why more structured testing is needed:

1   You have no proof of this testing and the exam board needs evidence in the form of a test plan, a table of tests carried out and hardcopy evidence of the results.

2   Although each block of code may work individually, there may be bugs that arise as a result of the effect of one piece of code on another. Therefore, some whole system tests are needed.

3   Basic testing usually involves checking that the code works as expected. This means that it is only being tested with normal data. Tests with invalid and extreme data are needed to provoke failure. In other words you need to try to break your own system.

4   Your system may be technically superb and have no bugs in it at all. However, it may not actually do what the user wants it to. Therefore, acceptance testing is needed to check that the system meets all of the users' objectives.

System maintenance

Maintenance is the documentation needed to allow another person to understand your system. Many computer systems are written by a programmer and then handed over to the person or organisation that will use them. The maintenance documentation allows the person or organisation to correct any errors or add to the system if necessary.

It might help to think about open-source code which is currently very popular. Open source means that, as well as buying (or downloading) the software, the user is also given access to the source code so that they can adapt it for their own use. The Linux operating system is perhaps the best example of this. The source code is only useful if there is documentation that explains how it works. Similarly, whoever takes on the maintenance of your system will need to know how to maintain it.

It is important from the start of your project that you create it with this in mind. There is no point writing code that only makes sense to you – other people must be able to understand it. This means creating code in a structured way, using sensible naming conventions and annotating your code as you go along.

User Manual

The user manual is a document that explains how to use your system. It is designed for your user and must be written in a style that is appropriate to them. Typically, this will include an introduction to the system and details of how to install it. After that, a series of screen-grabs and 'how to' instructions should make up the main part of the document. Common errors and how to recover from them should also be included.

This section requires a sample rather than a full user guide. Although this is a relatively straightforward section, it can be very time-consuming to produce good user documentation.

Appraisal

An appraisal is an evaluation of how well you and your user think the project has gone. You wrote a list of objectives in the analysis section. You now need to go through each of these in turn, describing how you met each one. Where you didn't meet the objective, you should explain why not.

This section should also include suggestions for improvements. This might be aspects that you could have done better, or further functionality that you think should be added. Genuine feedback from your user should be included at this stage.

Remember that although this is the last stage of the life cycle for you, in real life it would feed in to the analysis of the next trip around the life cycle. In other words, this is the start of Version 2 of your system.

Assessment of coursework

The A2 project provides you with a realistic idea of how systems are created in real life. However, you are doing it primarily to get a good A level grade, so you need to keep an eye on the mark scheme at all times. Specific guidance on how to interpret the mark scheme is included in each section. At this stage it is worth pointing out the following:

○ The majority of the marks are for the first three sections: Analysis (12 marks), Design (12 marks) and Technical Solution (15 marks).
○ Many students are too keen to start the Technical Solution and do not spend enough time on the Analysis and Design sections.

○ Many students spend too much of their total time on the Technical Solution even though it is only worth 23% of the marks.

○ Many students run out of time and rush the User Manual and Appraisal, missing out on relatively easy marks. Set yourself some mini-deadlines for each section.

○ Programmed solutions do not have to be as 'slick' as database solutions. Students who choose to use a database package, such as Access, have an easier time when it comes to the Technical Solution and have more time to spend on the user interface.

The example project

Units 16–24 will take you through each of the stages of the life-cycle in some detail. Most of this information can be applied to any project, but on occasions, it is helpful to show parts of a real project. We will be using an expanded version of *Alice's Chocolates* that was first introduced in Unit 5. A summary of the company's broad requirements is shown below and the examples in the following units will refer to these requirements.

Case Study: Alice's Chocolates *overview*

Alice's Chocolates is a small company that makes and sells expensive chocolates via mail order. There is a production line on which the company produces six different varieties of chocolate. There are no plans to extend the product range. Customers can order as many as they want of each type and it is quite common for the company to receive large orders.

Alice owns the company and is in charge of all aspects of the management of the company, including the stock control and invoicing systems, although there are office staff who will also use the system.

They have a relatively small number of customers (around 50 at present) whose details are currently stored on index cards. When a new customer places an order, a new card is created. If any of the existing customer's details change, they write a new card and the old one is destroyed. There are some customers who have not placed orders for several months but Alice keeps their details in the card index just in case.

A printed invoice is sent to the customer that includes customer name and address, the description and individual cost of each product, the quantity sold and the total price including postage and packing. One copy of the invoice is printed and sent with the order. A second copy is stored in a file in the office.

They have no record of the levels of stock of finished products. Once a week, Alice checks the stock levels. When they are running short of a particular product, they will make more of that product on their production line. On occasions they do run out of stock, which means that customers have to wait a few days for their orders.

When they do run low on a particular product, they always make a set amount. This is called the 're-order level' and is different for each of the six types of chocolate they make because some types are more popular than others. They do not know exactly how many of each product they sell although this information would be useful to them. They sometimes change the re-order level if they need to, because they do not want to have excessive numbers of chocolates made up.

At the moment, the invoicing is done using a basic spreadsheet package. Alice types in all of the customer details from the index cards and then includes details of the order placed. The stock control is not computerised at all.

Alice is aware that there is software that will help her to run her business properly, but is not convinced that it will do exactly what she wants. She has asked you to look into the possibility of creating a system for her.

 Unit 15 Project ideas

The best projects have a real user with a real problem and this should be the starting point for your coursework. The exam board does not necessarily expect your real user to adopt your new system and use it in their organisation, but they do expect the user and the scenario to be real.

It is a requirement of AQA that the project involves the input, storage and manipulation of data and the output of results. This means that the project must involve data processing in some way. Due care should be taken to ensure that this requirement is met. For example, it might be interesting to create a website with animated graphics and sound but, unless it is linked to data handling in some way, it will score very few marks on the mark scheme.

It is important to find a topic that you have an interest in. You will live with this project for most of the academic year so if you choose a very dry topic you may regret it later on. Also, try to choose something that is open ended as this can score more highly than a project that is very narrow in scope.

Where to get your project ideas

Work experience

Most students have at least one week of work experience. Is there anything you can do based around yours? Are you still in touch with anyone who could now act as your user? Even if they already have a computer system is there anything that could be done to improve it? Did you see any opportunities to introduce a computer system?

Parents/Relatives

Is there anything that could be done for your parents'/relatives'/friends' work? Could they act as your user? Could they put you in touch with someone at their place of work who could?

Hobbies/Interests

Are you involved in any clubs or societies that could computerise their system? Could you use the club manager as your user?

Part-time/holiday work

Do you have a part-time job or do any casual work? Can your employer act as your user?

Teachers

If you draw a blank on all of the sources listed above, do any of your teachers have any requirements for a computer system? Could you create educational software for children lower down the school?

School administration

Are there any aspects of the school that could be computerised? Could one of the office staff become your user?

Ideas for projects

Below we list a number of projects that have been used successfully over the last five years. Each one of the them has a real user, which was fundamental to its success. The source of the idea is shown, along with the user and a rating as to the overall complexity of the problem.

Share club

Where did the idea come from?   Student's father
Who is the user?   Father and one other club member

A student's father was a member of a share club with around ten members. Each member invested £500, which meant that they had £5000 to invest on the stock market. The members met each month to look at their shares portfolio and decide whether to sell their shares and/or buy new stock.

The system allowed the user to enter the new share value of the shares that they owned and to track the performance over time. A graphing function was added so that members could easily interpret the data. The output from the system was used at their monthly meetings.

Complexity: *Easy/Fair*   Not too much data to enter, though the graphing functionality was new to both student and teacher.

Bus allocation

Where did the idea come from?   Deputy Head (via computing teacher)
Who is the user?   Deputy Head

A secondary school in a rural area has many students who travel in by bus. There are around 15 different bus routes, some of which have their own dedicated routes and some of which serve the same villages. For example, one village has three bus routes going through it. Each year, the Deputy Head has to allocate bus passes to the students. This involves ensuring that every student has a place reserved on a bus.

Complexity: *Fair/Hard*   Lots of data to enter and lots of relationships within the data.

Forklift truck

Where did the idea come from?   Computing teacher
Who is the user?   Computing teacher and Year 7, 8 and 9 pupils

All ICT teachers are required to teach their students how to use computer control. This is sometimes done in D&T lessons, where computers are programmed to control robots or Lego machines. In this case, the school could not afford to buy this equipment so the student was given the task of creating an educational package that taught the basics of computer control using a visual interface.

The teacher suggested a forklift truck simulation, where the truck moves around within a grid, putting and taking items from shelves. Commands can be entered into the system to control the truck – for example, FWD 4, RIGHT 90, GET3 and so on. The student added 3D graphics to show what the forklift truck was doing as it followed the students' instructions.

Complexity: *Hard*   This was a very able student. They added a number of additional features which were not specified by the user and used a 3D graphics package that they had at home.

Shape recognition software

Where did the idea come from?   Student's mother who is a primary school teacher.
Who is the user?   Student's mother and a selection of Year 2 students

A simple program was written that randomly produced 2D shapes. The user was prompted to select the name of the shape from a drop-down list. A message displayed whether the pupil had chosen correctly or not. A text box displayed the number of correct answers. The system operated on two levels, with more complex shapes being used on the higher level.

In addition to the program itself, which was quite simple, a teacher module was added which kept track of the pupil's names and scores and started them on the most appropriate level.

Complexity: *Easy/Fair*   The shape recognition was straightforward, though the storing of scores was slightly more complex. A more able student could extend this idea considerably. Recognising shapes on its own was not enough as the data handling was very limited. It was the addition of a teacher module that made it more appropriate.

Grain management system

Where did the idea come from?   Work experience on father's farm
Who is the user?   Farm manager

A farmer stores his own and other farmers' grain in a number of large grain stores and silos on the family farm. The grain goes though a drying process which takes several weeks and involves moving the grain from one storage facility to another.

The temperature and moisture content of the grain are continually monitored so that the farm manager knows at what point to move it from one part of the farm to another and at what point it can be collected ready for sale.

The system required a number of readings to be entered and then, using a system of rules, advised the user on what to do next. This might involve moving the grain, increasing the temperature or arranging delivery.

Complexity: *Easy*   A simple knowledge-based system that looks at the data input and advises on what to do. A simple user interface needed.

The scope of the coursework

The complexity of a project is a major consideration. Remember that you will be developing this system largely on your own. It is probably not a good idea to take on a problem that you do not think you will be able to solve in the time. On the other hand, you don't want a project that only involves a limited number of skills. Select a project that fits around your level of expertise with VB. You would expect to have to learn some new aspects of VB, but you don't want every line of code to be a challenge.

Consider the amount of data that you want to handle. The final solution must be a fully working system, so working with a small sample of data may not be enough. The bus allocation system described above involved many repetitive functions being carried out on large volumes of data. This added to the total time spent on the project, without necessarily adding to the marks. On the other hand, the grain management system described above involved too little data and was limited as a result.

It cannot be stressed enough how important it is to have a real user with a real problem. It is also vital that you refer to your user at every stage of the project.

⊕ Unit 16 Analysis

Background information

Many students find this one of the most difficult parts of the coursework. This is usually because they don't have a real user or because they are trying to write the background information before speaking to the user.

The background information should introduce the person or organisation for whom you are creating the solution along with the main user or users. The existing system (whether computerised or not) should be explained in this section and there should be an analysis of the problem. This will help you to understand all of the problems that you will be facing including the volume of data involved, timescales and what processing will need to be carried out. You may find it helpful to split this into two discrete sections: **Background information** and **Description of the problem**. Most of this information needs to come from the user.

There are a number of techniques available for collecting the information. You can:

- Interview the user(s)
- Hand out a questionnaire to the user(s)
- Observe the current system
- Examine existing documents

Interview / questionnaire

The first thing you should do is interview your user. This might be difficult to do especially if you don't know them particularly well. Interviewing your parents is also fraught with problems as it may end up being a 'chat' with no real structure. You should plan what you are going to ask them and write down their answers or tape them so that you can transcribe the interview later.

The following questions could be applied to any project. You should customise these to your own requirements:

- How do you complete the task at the moment?
- What data do you have to put in to the current system?
- What happens to the data in the system?
- What information do you get out of the current system?
- What format is the output from the system?
- What are the good points of the current system?
- What are the problems with the current system?
- What features would you like the new system to have?
- How would you measure the success of a new system?

○ What has prompted you to consider having a new system?
○ Who will be using the system and what is their level of expertise?
○ What hardware do you have at present?

You could carry out the same exercise as a questionnaire, which is particularly useful if you have more than one user, as you can collect the data more quickly than by doing a series of interviews. However, this will not allow you to probe for more information and you may end up making assumptions about their answers.

There is a problem with users and that is that they don't really know what they want from a new system until they see it. If you tell the user that you are going to design a new system from scratch and that they can specify whatever features they like, they will probably find it really difficult. However, once you show them your first designs, they will have a lot to say. Therefore, this should be the first of many discussions you have with your user.

Observation of the current system

You should try to observe the system being used. If it is a computerised system, you could ask someone to explain it as they use it or get a copy of the software and use it yourself.

Observing the current system will help you to answer many of the same questions as an interview, but it is a more objective way of gathering information. For example, the user may consider that they have good ICT skills, whereas your observation might tell you otherwise. You may also observe some inefficiencies in the current method that the user simply does not notice, because they have been doing it that way for a long time.

If you are computerising a paper-based system, then remember the GIGO principle – Garbage In Garbage Out. What this means in this sense is that if the paper-based system does not work properly, then computerising it will lead to a computerised system that doesn't work properly either. It is important to focus on what you are hoping to achieve with the new system, rather than repeating the faults in the existing one.

Examination of existing documents

Your project should include examples of any input or output documents that are used in the current system. For example, if the user inputs data from a paper-based form, then you should include a copy of the form. More likely, you will be able to get hold of the documents that are the output of the current system. This might include completed order forms, invoices or any other document designed to be printed and taken out of the system.

You may include copies of this documentation in the body of your report. For example, you could scan the documents and then use them to identify data sources and destinations. You may include copies of the documents in an appendix. If you do use appendices, make sure that you clearly explain what the documents are and where they can be found in this section.

These documents are particularly useful in identifying the data items that are used and what happens to the data within the system. This will make it easier to create the Data Flow Diagrams (DFDs) required in this section.

Feasibility study

A feasibility study examines possible methods of solving the problem and considers which of these is the best suited to the problem. These solutions range from doing nothing at all and keeping the current system, through to getting a professional programmer to write a bespoke solution. You should also consider other ways in which you could create a solution. For example, is a programmed solution the best way? Could you create a database instead? If you are going to program it, then is VB the best program to use? Would a non-computerised system be more appropriate?

This is a bit if a hoop-jumping exercise as we already know that you will be programming the solution. If you weren't, then you could not do your coursework. However, you should still produce a serious and realistic feasibility study of all the alternatives.

This is the first time in the project where you consider the solution. You should not have mentioned the solution before this point. If you have made reference to solving the problem in VB you should go back and change it. You don't even know whether it is feasible to create a new system yet, let alone in VB.

The feasibility study itself could be done as a list of possible solutions, each followed by a brief description and a list of the advantages and disadvantages of that method. You can break it down into a series of steps. Again, you should customise this list to suit your own project:

1 Consider the overall solution

○ Stay with the current system
○ Modify the existing system (even if it is paper-based)
○ Create a new system

2 Consider who will develop the new system

Assuming that you decide to create a new system, you could then move on to possible solutions:

○ Pay a programmer to write a bespoke solution
○ Buy an off-the-shelf package and adapt it
○ Create a solution yourself

3 Consider which tools to use to create the solution

Assuming that you are going to create the new system yourself, you can move on to considering different programs:

○ Write it in Access or a similar database package
○ Write it using VB
○ Write it using another programming language

The final stage of the feasibility study is to summarise the reasons why you have chosen the method that you have.

Identifying objectives and acceptable limitations

It is very important, at this stage, to identify the scope of the problem. This means that you are very clear about what the system will do and what it is not expected to do. The best way to identify this is as a list of objectives. There is no set number of objectives that a project should have, but it is likely to range somewhere between six and twenty, depending on how specific they become. It is useful to split objectives between general and specific. All your objectives should be measurable so that you can assess your success later on.

General objectives

General objectives are broad in scope. Some of these could be applied to almost any project. For example:

○ To create a fully working solution
○ To meet the requirements of the user
○ To test the system to ensure that it works correctly

Specific objectives

Specific objectives tend to be more detailed and relate directly to the individual project. For example, *Alice's Chocolates* might have the following:

○ To create a printable invoice
○ To record the number sold, description, price, postage and packing and total cost of an order
○ To store the details for six types of chocolate
○ To store the details of each customer
○ To be able to change the current stock level, restock level and the type of chocolate
○ To view the current stock levels
○ To decrease the stock levels as chocolates are sold
○ To print a stock level report showing all products
○ To keep a record of each customer's orders

Limitations

You should also include any limiting factors at this stage. These are likely to be very specific to your project and include aspects that are outside the scope of the project. For example, *Alice's Chocolates* limitations might be:

○ It is not required to store details of more than six products.

○ Re-ordering of stock is done manually, so an automatic ordering system is not required.

○ Assume that the company only sells in the UK, so the system does not have to cope with international addresses or currency.

Data Flow Diagrams (DFDs)

There are a number of diagrams that you should complete as part of your project. Diagrams are a very useful way of organising your own thoughts and of explaining them to someone else in a clear way.

DFDs are a diagrammatical method of showing the source and destination of different items of data. It does not matter at this stage *how* the system processes the data, what is important here is *what* data is processed.

You may produce several levels of DFD, with each one being more detailed than the one before. It is usually sufficient to show a **context diagram** (also known as a Level 0 DFD) which shows an overview of the main processes and external entities.

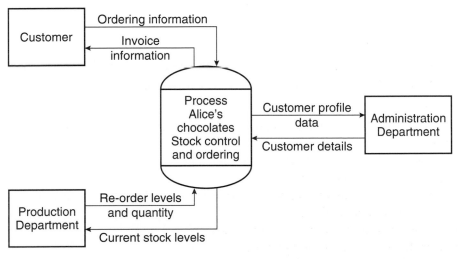

Figure 16.1 Context diagram for *Alice's Chocolates*

This can then be broken down further into a Level 1 DFD as shown in Figure 16.2

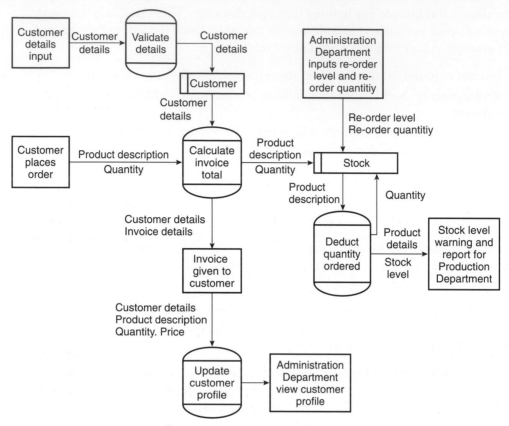

Figure 16.2 Level 1 Data Flow Diagram for Alice's Chocolates

Unit 17 Overall system design

Many students make the mistake of jumping straight from the **Analysis** into the **Implementation**, leaving the **Design** work until the end. Their logic is that they can simply document what they have done at the end. The problem with this approach is that the **Implementation** will take much longer if the design work is not done first. A further problem is that the unplanned design may not work, which they may not discover until it is too late. Unplanned work always takes longer.

Design involves several stages which are split up over the next three units. This unit covers the higher-level planning, including system flowcharts, structure diagrams, identifying the modular structure of the system and suitable algorithms that could be used. Units 18–19 cover the definition of data requirements, the user interface design and all other aspects of design.

System flowchart

It is important, from an early stage, to have an overall view of the design of the system. System flowcharts show this in a diagrammatical way. The idea is that the chart provides an overview, rather than the detail, of how the system will work. If you are creating a large system, it may be preferable to produce a series of flowcharts – one for each of the main processes you will be carrying out. It is sometimes easier to start a system flowchart by writing down the sequence that a user would go through when using the proposed system.

For example, a user of the *Alice's Chocolates* system who wanted to process an incoming order would go through the following sequence:

- Input the customer's name and address.
- Select the type of chocolate ordered.
- Input the quantity ordered.
- Calculate the total cost of the order, including postage and packing.
- Print the invoice.
- Deduct quantity from the current stock level which is stored in a file with a re-order level and re-order amount.
- Generate a warning if the stock levels is below the re-order level for that product.
- Produce a stock report showing the current stock levels of all products.

This can then be transferred into a system flow chart:

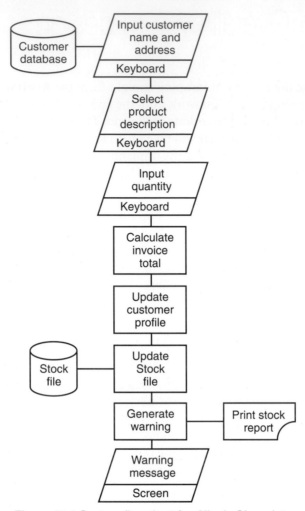

Figure 17.1 System flowchart for *Alice's Chocolates*

Structure diagrams

Another way of showing an overview of a system, is to produce a structure diagram. These work a bit like a family tree. You start with the whole program at the top and each level below shows a further detail of the components and processes that make up the system. There are a number of different ways of producing these charts, one of which is Jackson Structured Programming (JSP). This looks like a standard hierarchy chart, using a top-down approach, with each level set up from left to right showing the overall sequence.

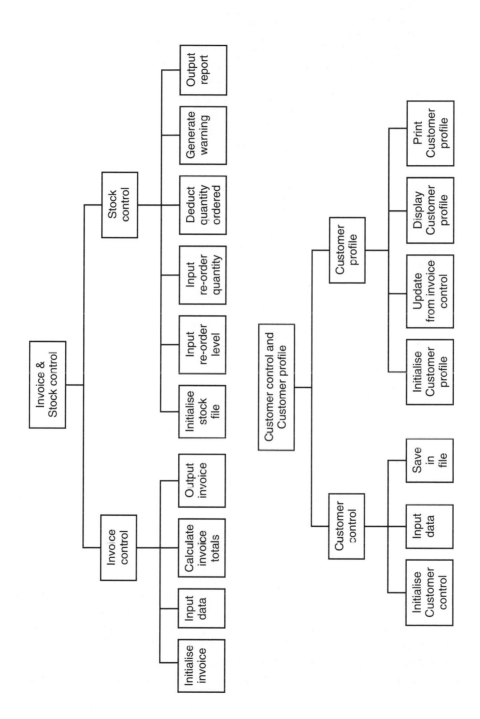

Figure 17.2 JSP diagram for
Alice's Chocolates

Modular structure

In this section, you should identify the main processes involved in creating the solution. Each main process will be a module or procedure in VB, that is, a block of code. In VB terms, these are the lines of code contained within the `Private Sub..End Sub` statements within a program. VB calls these procedures or sub-routines. You can also produce stand-alone modules which are stored separately within a VB program, which can be called from within a procedure wherever it is needed. Sub-routines are written to perform specific tasks, whereas modules can be used for common procedures which you may need in various parts of the program, for example, loading the details from a file.

By this stage, you should have a clearer idea of the sub-routines and modules that you will need to write and how they will fit together. At a simple level, it may be that each symbol in the system flowchart, or each box in a structure diagram, will require a corresponding routine to make it happen.

For example with *Alice's Chocolates* you may have sub-routines for the following:

- Initialise the form with text boxes and control buttons
- Calculate product price from product description
- Calculate the invoice total
- Print the invoice
- Initialise the stock control file with stock levels, re-order levels and re-order quantity
- Pass the quantity sold into the stock file
- Deduct quantity sold from stock level
- Generate a warning
- Print stock report

Identification of suitable algorithms

Ultimately, you will need to break the problem down into steps that can be converted into program constructs. These might include concepts such as:

- Assignment – allocating a value
- Selection – If/Then and Select/Case
- Iteraton – Do Until, While…Loop , For…Next

You should identify the types of statements that you will be using within your solution. You do not have to produce 100% accurate VB statements at this stage and you do not need to write out all of the code that you plan to use. Instead, you should write the main algorithms that you intend to use in pseudo-code.

For example, with *Alice's Chocolates*:

Calculate the total cost of an order

```
Set the grand total to zero
   In a loop
       Read the number required
     Read the unit cost
     Calculate the total for this type of chocolate
     Add to the grand total
     End the loop
Add postage and packing costs
Display totals on screen
```

Update the customer file

```
Open Customer File
   If Customer details have changed Then
     Update Customer details
   Else Do Nothing
Save File
```

Generate a low stock warning

```
Identify stock Item
Subtract quantity ordered from stock level
If stock level is less than re-order level then
   Generate warning message
Else Do Nothing
Record new stock level
```

As you can see, you do not need to be concerned about the detail at this stage, just the main constructs. You should produce a block of pseudo-code for each of the main procedures.

Unit 18 Definition of data requirements and validation

> In this section, you should list every item of data that you will be using, including the name of the item and the data type. You should also consider the way in which data will be stored in files, the way in which data is entered into the system and what impact this may have on the way in which the data capture process is designed. For example, if keyboard entry is the main form of data input, you should consider all the methods of validation that could be applied.

Record and data structures

VB supports a number of built-in data types. Data types are assigned to variables when the variables are declared.

The most common data types are shown below. along with their properties

DATA TYPE	PROPERTIES
String	Any keyboard characters
Integer	Whole numbers between −32,768 and 32,767
Single and Double	Real numbers – i.e. with decimal points
Boolean	True or False as −1 and 0
Date	Date fields

Where built-in data types are used, it is not always necessary to explain in your project why you have chosen the particular types, providing you have chosen the most appropriate data type for the data being stored. It would, however, be worth explaining why you have chosen **Integer** or **Real** for storing numbers.

You may have defined your own data structures. If this is the case, you should describe how these have been constructed. *Alice's Chocolates* uses three user-defined data types to store customer, stock and invoice details.

These could be shown as follows:

- **CustomerDetails** is made up of:
  - CustName As String * 40
  - CustAddress As String * 200
  - CustPhone As String * 20
  - CustEmail As String * 100

- **StockStructure** is made up of:
  - StockName As String * 20
  - StockCurrent As Integer
  - StockReStock As Integer
  - StockPrice As Integer

- **InvoiceStructure** is made up of:
  - InvoiceCustID As Integer
  - InvoiceDate As Date
  - InvoiceQuantity(6) As Integer
  - InvoiceCost(6) As Integer
  - InvoicePaP As Single
  - InvoicePaid As Boolean

Values in brackets indicate that an array is being used, with six elements in each array. These relate to the six product items that *Alice's Chocolates* stocks and sells.

File organisation and processing

It is likely that you will be using data files to read data in and out of your program. All programs will involve the input, process and output of data. The **process** part has already been explained in previous sections, as this will be the actions that take place on the data as defined by your procedures.

The input of data may all come initially from keyboard entry or from a file. Some files are used to input data to the system and to store the data coming out.

The stock control file is a good example of this in the *Alice's Chocolates* system. The user will set this file up initially by inputting values via a form. After this, the values stored will change as a result of orders being placed through the invoicing system.

In your coursework, you should identify what files will be used, what the file structure will be and why you have chosen that structure. You should also explain what the files are used for and the links between them.

In *Alice's Chocolates* three random access files are used: **CustomerFile**, **InvoiceFile** and **StockFile**.

Identifying variables and constants

It is good practice, when programming, to identify every variable and constant that you will be using throughout the program. A variable is any item of data where the value may change as the program is run. A constant is a value that does not change.

VB supports a number of data types and you should choose the most appropriate and efficient for the job. VB also allows you to create your own data types. If you intend to do this, then you must explain it in this section.

Produce a list of variables identifying which are local (only used within one procedure) or global (used throughout the whole program) and state what each variable/constant is going to be used for. You may find it easier to list the global variables and then produce a list of variables for each form and module.

An extract of a list of variables is shown below for two of the forms used in *Alice's Chocolates*:

FrmCustomerControl

VARIABLE NAME	TYPE	LOCAL/GLOBAL
CustomerDetails	User-defined data type called CustomerStructure	Local
CustCurrentRecord	Integer	Local/Global
CustRecordCount	Integer	Global
CustChangeFlag	Boolean	Local/Global
ErrorType	Integer	Local Local

o **CustomerDetails** is a user-defined variable using a user defined variable type. It is a bit like an array – it is one variable that has many of parts or elements. In this case it has four – customer name, address, telephone number and email address. This is defined in a module and is set up as a global variable, which means it can be used anywhere in the program.
o **CustCurrentRecord** is used to store the number of the customer record that is currently being displayed. This is a whole number.
o **CustRecordCount** is used to store the number of records in the file. This is a whole number.
o **CustChangeFlag** is used to indicate if any changes have been made to a record. If they have, the user will be prompted to save if any attempt is made to leave the record. This is either True or False.
o **ErrorType** is used to record the user's response to a 'Do you want to save?' option. There may be several options which is why it is set to integer.

FrmStockControl

VARIABLE NAME	TYPE	LOCAL/GLOBAL
StockDetails	User-defined data type called StockStructure	Global
InvoiceDetails	User-defined data type called InvoiceStructure	Global
StockCounter	Integer	Local
StockChangeFlag	Boolean	Local
ErrorType	Integer	Local
InvoiceCount	Integer	Local
DateFirst	Date	Local
DateLast	Date	Local

○ **StockDetails** and **InvoiceDetails** used to read details from the **Stock** and **Invoice** files respectively. These are both user-defined data types.
○ **StockStructure** is made up of three arrays, each with seven elements, though only six elements will be used. These are also been defined globally in a module:
  StockName As String * 20
  StockCurrent As Integer
  StockReStock As Integer
  StockPrice As Integer
○ **StockCounter** is used as the counter in a For/Next loop and is a whole number.
○ **StockChangeFlag** is used to indicate if any changes have been made. This flag is checked before the fork is exited. This is either True or False so is set to Boolean.
○ **ErrorType** is used in conjunction with the flag detailed above to see if the user wants to save the changes made. There may be several answers, so it is set to integer.
○ **OutOfMessage** stores details of any stock that has gone below the pre-set re-stock levels. It stores the name of the item and is therefore a string.
○ **InvoiceCount** is used as a counter in a loop that works through all the invoices. This loop is used to calculate sales for a given time period. This is a whole number.
○ **DateFirst** and **DateLast** store the first and last dates used across all the invoices that have been saved.

Data entry and validation

At this stage, you should consider what validation can be applied to the data that a user might enter. You do not need to explain how it will be coded at this stage. There are six main validation techniques:

○ **Type check** ensures that data entered is of a specific type – e.g. text, numeric (quantity ordered must be numeric).

- o **Range check** ensures that data entered is within a specified numeric range – e.g. quantity ordered must be between 1 and 1000.
- o **Character count** ensures that data entered is greater than or less than a set number of characters or digits – e.g. customer name cannot be more than 30 characters; password must have 8 characters.
- o **Look-up check** checks data entered against a pre-defined list. The most common implementation of this within VB is the use of a drop-down list. Checking the password entered against the correct password stored in a file is another example.
- o **Format check** ensures that data follows a set pattern. These are sometimes called **input masks**. For example, currency must be in the format £00.00; date must be in the format dd/mm/yy.
- o **Presence check** ensures that there must be some data entered into the control – i.e. it cannot be left blank.

You should also consider what action to take if any of the validation rules are broken. Again, the specific code required does not need to be considered yet but you should think about useful error messages that you can apply. For example, if the user enters 1,000,000 for the quantity ordered, the error message may read '**Please input a value between 1 and 1000**'.

Validation will only work on data that the user enters – it will not work on data that is calculated as part of the program.

The variables and validation checks could be shown as one table or as a series of tables, one per form. An extract of the *Stock control* form for *Alice's Chocolates* is shown below:

VARIABLE NAME	TYPE	VALIDATION	COMMENTS
CustomerDetails	User-defined	None	Made up from customer name, address, telephone number and email address
CustName	String * 40	Presence check	Error message: "Customer name cannot be left blank"
CustAddress	String * 200	Presence check	Error message: "Customer address cannot be left blank"
CustPhone	String * 20		Details are non-essential
CustEmail	String * 100		Details are non-essential
CustCurrentRecord	Integer	None	Displays current customer number
ErrorType	Integer	Select from list: Yes, No , Cancel	
DateFirst	Date	Presence check	Error message: "Date cannot be left blank".
DateLast		Format check	Error message: "Please enter a date in the following format ##/##/##"

Security and integrity of data

You should consider appropriate measures for ensuring the security and integrity of your data. **Security** is ensuring that the data cannot be accessed by unauthorised users. **Integrity** is ensuring that once data is entered into the system, it cannot become corrupt in any way.

The measures that you propose for your system must be appropriate to the situation. If you were creating a system to handle on-line banking transactions, then security would be a key issue. If you are creating a stock control system for a chocolate manufacturer, it is not that important. It is worth noting that if personal details are being stored, as is the case with *Alice's Chocolates*, then the company must register with the Data Protection Registrar and abide by their regulations relating to the security of data. Therefore, they do have a legal responsibility to store the data securely.

In most cases, it is sufficient to have password protection on the system. You may choose to password-protect specific files, or set up different levels of access for different users. Some files could be set to **read-only**. You may also want to consider aspects of physical security, such as controlled access to computers facilities.

Equally important is a recovery plan in the event of loss of data. You may want to include this as one of the objectives for the project. To take the two examples above, an on-line bank may do real-time back-ups, taking copies of every single transaction. In the case of *Alice's Chocolates* a daily back-up would be sufficient.

If you do suggest a password system, then you will need to implement it in your final solution. All other aspects of security should be described in your coursework documentation.

In the case of *Alice's Chocolates*, a password is required to access the system and the user needs to be able to change this password as required.

Planning a test strategy

At this stage, you do not need to describe the testing in detail. You will do this later. In this section, you should explain what tests you plan to do, identifying the test data you intend to use. It is important that your tests are designed to provoke failure as well as testing the system under normal operation.

There are several different types of test that you should plan for. You should customise your test plan to suit your project:

Functional testing

Every text box should have three types of test data typed into it:

○ **Normal:** data it is expected to handle
○ **Invalid:** data outside the range of normal expected data, including data that is deliberately wrong – e.g. inputting text in a number field
○ **Boundary:** data that is on the boundary of acceptability – e.g. if quantity has a range check between 1 and 100, you should test 0,1, 100 and 101.

In addition, every event (e.g. clicking on a button, tabbing or pressing the ENTER key) should be checked to ensure it functions as expected.

Unit testing

Every procedure should be tested to ensure that it does what it is supposed to. This can be done in two ways:

○ **Black box:** Check the outcome produced by the system with a different method – e.g. check calculations by comparing the results using a calculator.
○ **White box:** Check each individual step of a process to ensure it is working correctly. This is like a dry-run of the system.

System testing

You need some 'whole system' tests that check that the system meets its objectives. For example, with *Alice's Chocolates* you might produce an order for a new customer. This would effectively check the whole system.

Acceptance testing

You need to involve your user in the testing process. If possible, you should get them to carry out the system testing before you deliver the final system. This is known as beta testing and often identifies bugs that were not spotted before, as the system is being used 'in anger'.

The best way to document this is to produce the outline of a test plan. This is time well spent, as you can then use the same table to complete the **Testing** section of your coursework. The extract below shows the test that could be planned for the **Invoicing** component of *Alice's Chocolates*:

TEST NUMBER	DESCRIPTION OF TEST	TEST DATA	EXPECTED OUTCOME
1	Enter valid data into txtCustomerID	2	Accept
2	Enter invalid data into txtCustomerID	Cheese	Error message
3	Enter valid date into txtInvoiceDate	12/04/04	Accept
4	Enter invalid data into txtInvoiceDate	120901	Error message
...			
20	Check calculation in txtChocsOrdered	Add '3' into Quantity ordered in Invoice form	TxtStockCurrent should decrease by 3
21	Check calculation in txtInvoiceTotalMoney	Input values in txtSubtotal array: 0.12, 0.26, 0.42, 0.60, 0.80, 1.02	3.22
22	Check calculation in txtInvoiceTotalGrand	Total = £3.22 + Post and Package £4.25	7.47
...			
34	Check command buttons: cmdFirst, cmdBack, cmdForward cmdEnd	Click buttons	Display first record Display previous record Display next record Display last record
35	Check cmdInvoiceNew command button	Click button	All text boxes should clear
36	Check cmdPrintInvoice command button	Click button	Invoice should print
37	Check cmdInvoiceSave command button	Click button	Invoice should save

As you can see from this extract, the number of tests that you could carry out is quite extensive, even on a relatively small program. It is not necessary to test every possible scenario. The exam board only require a sample of tests to prove that you have carried out a range of appropriate tests using suitable test data. Therefore, your table should include as many tests as are necessary to prove that your system is reliable and robust.

⊕ Unit 19 User interface design

In VB, the user interface design relates to the design of the forms, the error messages and the printed output that the program will use. These provide the link between the functionality of the program and the user. It is very important that these are designed prior to implementation rather than rushing into VB and dropping boxes and buttons around randomly. This means designing the forms and printed outputs using a word-processing or drawing package or even drawing them out by hand.

Form designs

Many programmers prefer to draw their designs by hand, as it tends to be quicker. The designs do not have to look particularly smart, as long as they show all of the design features. Your ideas will evolve as you develop the system and your user will probably make suggestions during the process as well. This means that the final system may look different to the original designs.

You will need to draw out the forms, showing all of the controls and features that will appear on them. There are only a limited number of controls that can be placed on a form, so you should consider which are the most appropriate for the task. For example, is it more appropriate to select an option from an option box, a check box, or a drop-down list?

Your main priority here should be the capabilities of the user. If you hide away the main functions in menus, a less able user may find your system harder to use. In this case, it may be preferable to have common functions attached to control buttons on the form. On the other hand, an experienced user may find big control buttons a bit clumsy and might prefer to use the system entirely through hot keys (ALT keys).

It is worth producing prototype designs for the user and requesting their feedback. This may sound like extra work but, as you are only producing the layout and not the code, it does not take long. In addition, if you develop the system based on designs that the user has not approved, they may reject your system when you deliver it or request changes that have many knock-on effects to the system you thought was finished.

This stage is concerned only with the contents and layout of the forms themselves. It is not necessary to explain in detail all the coding that will sit behind the forms. It is necessary to identify the controls that you will be using and the names that you will be assigning to them. You should use the standard naming convention described in Unit 2 and Appendix 2.

If you have a number of forms that are very similar, you could show the design for one of the forms and then list the other forms that have the same features.

You should consider the opening screen that you intend to use. The *Alice's Chocolates* program, for example, loads **FrmPasswordControl** and then opens **FrmInvoiceControl**. You, or rather your user, may choose to have a splash screen with a company logo and the name of the program. You could display this for a few seconds and set it to move on with a single click. Splash screens are often used to provide information on the screen while the program loads. However, there are no extra marks on the mark scheme for them, so don't spend too long designing them.

It may be appropriate to create a main screen which contains links to all of the other forms that you will be using. This is sometimes referred to as a **switchboard**. Your user may prefer this approach. Either way, it will be necessary to create links between all the forms that you create, so that the user can get to them.

Alice's Chocolates requires six forms:

○ **frmPasswordControl**: to enter the password
○ **frmPassword Change**: to change the password
○ **frmInvoiceControl**: to create invoices
○ **frmStockControl**: to keep track of stock levels
○ **frmCustomerControl**: to manage the customer details
○ **frmCustomerProfile**: to track customer's purchases and payments

The design of each form is quite different, so all six designs would be included if this was a real piece of coursework. One example is shown in Figure 19.1.

These designs are deliberately basic in order to identify a number of key features relating to the human computer interface (HCI).

There should be a common feel across the whole project. You should consider some or all of the following:

○ Overall form layout
○ Keeping common features in the same place on each form
○ Use of frames to group similar information
○ Navigation between forms
○ Size/shape of command buttons
○ Formatting for the title bar, labels and command button text
○ Formatting of data entered into text boxes
○ Positioning and size of forms on the screen
○ Disabling or 'low-lighting' features to stop the user changing details
○ Size of text boxes to allow for details such as addresses, passwords, tables and, in this case, the customer's order history which uses a scroll bar
○ Choice of words – e.g. do you use **Print** or **Print this Invoice**
○ Design of error messages

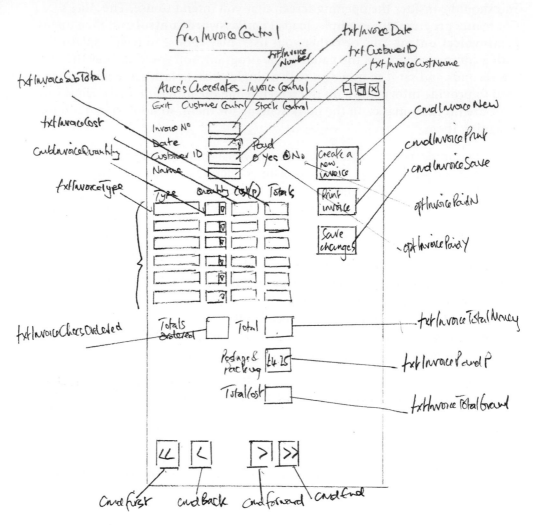

Figure 19.1 FrmInvoiceControl

You could explain some of your design choices either by describing them or by annotating your rough designs. This is an ideal opportunity to show that you have considered the user's requirements as part of the process. For example, if the system is educational software for young children, the design will be very different to an invoicing system for a big business.

There may also be hardware considerations. For example, if the user is running 800 x 600 screen resolution, you need to consider this in the design, especially if your PC has a higher resolution.

Printed output designs

Printed outputs have different design considerations, compared to an on-screen form. When you create a form, you have to consider the layout on the screen and how the user will interact with it. With printed output you are designing the layout of a document, probably onto an A4 sheet of paper. The dimensions of a computer screen and those of an A4 piece of paper are very different. Therefore, writing a program where you print the screen is unlikely to result in good quality output from the system.

You need to think carefully about what information is needed on the output and where you are going to put it on the page. Some of the information may be the same for every print-out and some will change. For example, *Alice's Chocolates* requires an invoice as one of its outputs. The invoice will contain some fixed information, for example, the company name, logo and address. It will also contain information that changes each time, for example, customer name and address, product ordered, quantity ordered and price. Your designs should reflect this.

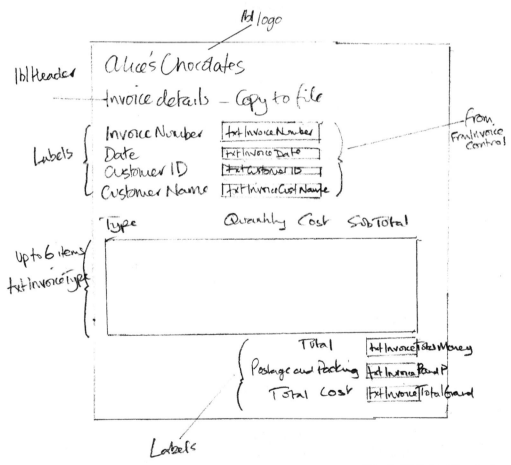

Figure 19.2 Invoice design

⊕ Unit 20 Technical solution

> The **Technical Solution** is the program itself. In theory, as all of the design work
> has been done, the Technical Solution should be the process of generating the
> forms and the VB code as per the design. In practice, it may not be quite this
> simple, as you may come across problems that were not anticipated at the design
> stage. Alternatively, the user may request changes or additions to the functionality
> as the project progresses.

Evidence required for the technical solution

You need to provide evidence that you have implemented your system effectively. You
will not be asked to send your finished program to the exam board. This is because
they allow you to program in any language you choose and they cannot expect their
moderators to have access to all of the possible programming languages that are
available.

Therefore, what they want to see is all of your VB code and a sample of the completed
forms. The sample you choose should show the solution in use, so the forms need to
contain 'real' data. There is some duplication here with the **System Maintenance**
which also requires you to show the **Technical Solution** of your system.

The difference between the two sections is that the **Technical Solution** proves that
your system has been created and works. The **System Maintenance** section is the
documentation that you would give to whoever will be looking after the system from
now on.

You do not need to provide the exam board with the same information twice.
Therefore, you can supply your VB code and examples of the completed forms in the
System Maintenance section. This means that you will not actually have a section in
your coursework for the technical solution.

How your solution is marked

Although the exam board will not test the system for real, your teacher is required to
authenticate the work and give it a mark based on the following:

○ **Structure** — is your system well-structured and efficient:
○ **Completeness** — does the system meet the specification or even exceed it:
○ **Technical competence** — have you demonstrated a good grasp of VB over a range
  of complex tasks?

The marks that they award usually fall into four categories. The higher the category, the more marks you will get in this section:

○ An unstructured program solving a trivial problem which may be incomplete or not working properly.
○ An unstructured program that solves a standard problem and produces some correct results.
○ A reasonably well-structured program that works and uses parameters and user-defined data structures.
○ A well-structured program that works fully and shows evidence of a range of programming techniques.

You should always bear in mind the number of marks that are available in this section. The 2005 Specification allocates just under 25% of the total project marks for the **Technical Solution**. You should think about the amount of time that you should allocate to writing code. In theory, you might allocate 25% of your total time to it though, in practice, the programming element is likely to take longer.

It is very common for students to rush the final four sections as they spend too much time completing and then tweaking the final solution. It is natural that you will want to 'crack' technical problems but keep an eye on the bigger picture – you are trying to get the highest possible mark in your coursework. You might spend several hours trying to perfect a small part of the program which, in the end, will add very few marks to your total. There are still 28 marks to be claimed in the sections that come after this, so allow sufficient time for these.

As with every section of your coursework you should try to involve the user. This could mean showing them samples of the forms as you create them or even getting them to trial sections of code as you complete them. They might make suggestions along the way that lead to a better solution. They may even save you some time. For example, if you are struggling with a particular piece of functionality, it may be that they are happy to have it delivered in a different way, which is easier for you to program.

The final thing to remember is that you may see other students working with databases, producing highly customised user interfaces that look very professional. VB solutions are not expected to be as 'slick' as more time and effort is spent setting up the structure of the program and the data, whereas databases have this set up already.

⊕ Unit 21 System testing

In the **Design** section, you were required to produce an outline of your test strategy. In this section, you are required to carry out the tests, document the results and provide evidence that you have carried out the tests.

Even a basic VB program could generate dozens of possible tests, so you need to be selective about which tests you show. This is actually good news, as you do not need to carry out repetitive tests that could take up a lot of your time.

A good plan would be to use all of the different approaches which will then prove that your system works fully. Remember that you are not just testing functionality, you are also testing that the system meets the users' objectives.

The test table

You could produce your results in a table as shown in the following extract:

TEST NUMBER	DESCRIPTION OF TEST	TEST DATA	EXPECTED OUTCOME	ACTUAL OUTCOME
1	Enter valid data into txtCustomerID	2	Accept	Accepted
2 Fig 21.1	Enter invalid data into txtCustomerID	Cheese	Error message	Error message
3	Enter valid date into txtInvoiceDate	12/04/04	Accept	Accepted
4	Enter invalid data into txtInvoiceDate	120901	Error message	Accepted
20	Check calculation in txtChocsOrdered	Add '3' into Quantity ordered in Invoice form	TxtStockCurrent should decrease by 3	TxtStockCurrent decreases by 3
21 Fig 21.2	Check calculation in txtInvoiceTotalMoney	Input values in txtSubtotal array: 0.12, 0.26, 0.42, 0.60, 0.80, 1.02	3.22	3.22
22 Fig 21.2	Check calculation in txtInvoiceTotalGrand	Total = £3.22 + Post and Package £4.25	7.47	7.47

34	Check command buttons: cmdFirst, cmdBack, cmdForward cmdEnd	Click buttons	 Display first record Display previous record Display next record Display last record	 Display first record Display previous record Display next record Display last record
35	Check cmdInvoiceNew command button	Click button	All text boxes should clear	All text boxes clear
36	Check cmdPrintInvoice command button	Click button	Invoice should print	Invoice prints
37	Check cmdInvoiceSave command button	Click button	Invoice should save	Invoice is saved

One of the problems you face here is that you probably tested your system as you went along. Typically, when you write a section of code, or add a control to a form you will automatically check that it works. If it doesn't work you will correct it straight away. This is perfectly acceptable. However, it means that when you carry out the testing at this stage, there will probably be very few errors. You might think that this looks at bit suspicious as there are no errors. If this is the case, then it would be worth explaining this in your write-up. Any errors that are recorded at this stage must be explained in the **Appraisal** section.

There is a temptation to 'fudge' testing claiming that you have done it when you haven't. It's important that you actually carry out testing properly and report any faults you find. You should also be very honest and, if you find errors, you should show them. In the example above, Test 4 produced an unexpected result in that an incorrect value was accepted. This has been shown and the 'corrective action' completed to show what has been done about it. This example also shows the importance of testing erroneous/invalid entries as well as valid ones. Don't forget to retest once you have corrected the fault.

Evidence required for testing

You need to provide evidence for a selection of your tests. The test plan shown above is an extract of one produced for *Alice's Chocolates*. It shows three different types of test:

○ Tests 1 to 4 check the input of data — whether the system allows invalid data to be entered.

○ Tests 20 to 22 check the processing of data – whether the algorithms produce the correct results.

○ Tests 34 to 37 are functional tests – they check whether the command buttons carry out the correct action.

It would be sufficient to select samples of these different types of test and then provide evidence that they have been carried out. Where possible, the evidence should be in the form of a print-out. You should annotate the print-out to explain the test clearly. For example, one print out might show valid data being entered into the system correctly, while another shows an error message generated when invalid data is entered. All tests should be cross-referenced to the test table using the test number.

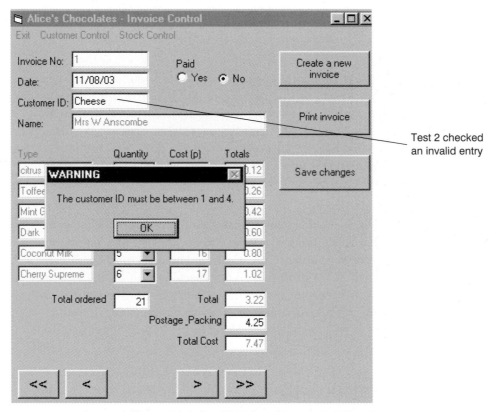

Figure 21.1 Sample of annotated test: Test 2

Notice that the error message is shown 'in situ' on top of the form from which it is generated.

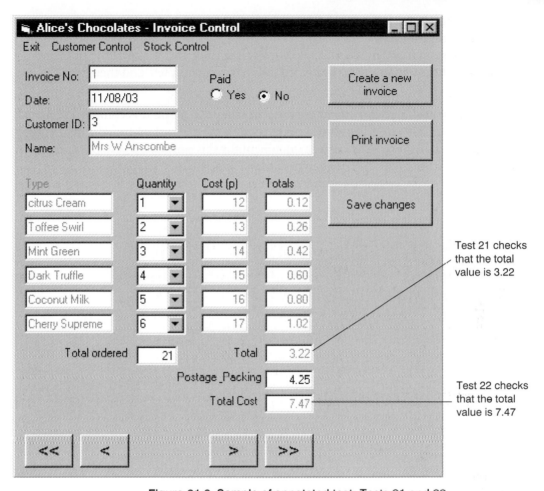

Figure 21.2 Sample of annotated test: Tests 21 and 22

Acceptance testing

The importance of the user has been stressed throughout and this section is no different. You may have produced a technically perfect system. However, if it is not what the user wanted, then it is useless. Acceptance testing means giving the system to your user and getting them to test it in a real environment.

Users often use software in ways that you have not anticipated. They may use a particular sequence of actions that you did not cover in your testing or they may even carry out unexpected actions that you had not planned for. The other thing they will do is tell you whether or not the system does what they want it to – that is, whether or not it meets the objectives.

You may choose to carry out some beta testing. This is where you give your user the program on the understanding that it is not quite finished and it may still contain bugs. This is often preferable, as it allows you time to put right any of the problems they find. The alternative is to wait until the system is complete and then give it to them to test.

Either way, you should document the tests that they carry out. It is common practice in the commercial world to get your client to 'sign off' the system to indicate that they are happy with it. You could create a document for this purpose, or ask the user to confirm in writing that they are happy with the system.

Unit 22 System maintenance

Once you have completed the system you will deliver it to your user and then they will continue to use it. In real life, if you are a programmer, you will then move onto your next project and probably have very little to do with the program ever again. This means that you must give your user everything they need to maintain the system.

There are three different types of maintenance:

○ **Perfective** – minor adjustments to make the system work exactly as required
○ **Adaptive** – adjustments made over time as the users' requirements change
○ **Corrective** – putting right any errors that get discovered in use

In order to carry out any type of maintenance on a VB program, your user will need the following:

1 Details of variables
2 Details of procedures/modules
3 Details of files and their structure
4 Annotated code listing
5 Hard copy of forms
6 Hard copy of outputs
7 An overview of the system

This unit explains what you should produce in each section, using examples from the completed *Alice's Chocolates* program. In your coursework, your maintenance section is likely to be one of the largest.

1 List of variables

This can be a print-out from VB, or you can create a table within your write-up, which lists all of the variables explaining how they have been declared and how they are used. In the example below, the global variables contained in the module are shown. The local variables are then shown for each form. In this example, we have only shown one form. Your coursework should include all the variables you have used.

Example list of variables

Module 1

```
Type CustomerStructure
   CustName As String * 40
   CustAddress As String * 200
   CustPhone As String * 20
   CustEmail As String * 100
End Type
```

FrmCustomerControl

VARIABLE	TYPE	HOW USED
CustomerDetails	User-defined	User-defined variable. It has four elements: customer name, address, telephone number and email address.
CustCurrentRecord	Integer	Stores the number of the customer record that is currently being displayed.
CustRecordCount	Integer	Stores the number of records in the file.
CustChangeFlag	Boolean	Used to indicate if any changes have been made to a record. If they have, the user will be prompted to save if any attempt is made to leave the record.
ErrorType	Integer	Used to record the user's response to a 'Do you want to save?' option.

2 List of procedures/modules

All of the main procedures should be listed with a brief explanation of their purpose.

Example list of procedures/modules

`Form_Load()`	Loads details that the other procedures will need, such as number of customer records.
`CustUpdate(Update)`	Updates the customer records.
`cmdSave_Click()`	Saves the currently displayed record to the customer file.
`cmdCustNew_Click()`	Clears the screen ready for a new customer's details to be added.

`txtCustName_Change()`
`txtCustAddress_Change()`
`txtCustPhone_Change(), _`
`txtCustEMail_Change()`
	Called if a change is made to any details of the currently displayed record.

`cmdStart_Click(), _`
`cmdBack_Click() _`
`cmdForward_Click(), _`
`cmdEnd_Click()`
	Deal with mouse clicks on the buttons to move through the customer records.

`cmdCustView_Click()`	Opens a form to show the customer's history details.

`mnuInvoice_Click(), _`
`mnuStock_Click()`
`mnuExit_Click()`
	Deal with mouse clicks on the menu bar options that access other areas of the program.

3 List of files

You must provide a list of the files that are read in or out of the program, showing where they are stored and what file types are used, as well as the structure of the data they contain.

Example list of files

NAME OF FILE	FILE LOCATION	FILE TYPE
Customerfile.txt	\Alicefiles	Random access file: CustName As String (40 characters) CustAddress As String (200 characters) CustPhone As String (20 characters) CustEmail As String (100 characters)
Invoicefile.txt	\Alicefiles	Random access file
Stockfile.txt	\Alicefiles	Random access file

4 Code listing

Your entire VB code should be printed out. It is essential that this is commented. You can do this in two ways. You can print the code and then annotate it by hand or, preferably, you will use the commenting feature in VB as shown in the extract below. It is not necessary to comment every single line of code. You should provide comments that would be useful to another person who will be maintaining your system from now on. In this example, each of the main procedures is explained using the comments. You should make sure your code is well laid out using conventions such as indenting loops, using gaps to highlight sections and using sensible names for the variables and procedures you have created.

Example of commented VB code

The following is a small extract of part of the code from the Customer Control form. Comments have been added to the code by adding a single apostrophe (') to the beginning of the line. This indicates that the text is a comment and VB will not attempt to execute it. VB will show comments in green, however, in the extract below, they are in *italics*.

```
'Find number of records in the file, calls the
 procedure CustUpdate using parameter 1 — forces the
 loading of the first record.
```

```
Private Sub Form_Load()
  Open "AliceFiles\CustomerFile.txt" For Random As #1 _
Len = 360
    CustRecordCount = LOF(1) / 360
  Close #1
  CustChangeFlag = False
  CustCurrentRecord = 1
  CustUpdate (1)
End Sub
```

'Checks for changes made to current record. If yes -
prompts for save using a message box.
'Update' loads details of relevant record from file.
Loads into user variable 'CustomerDetails', then put
into the correct text boxes in form.

```
Private Sub CustUpdate(Update)
  If CustChangeFlag = True Then
    ErrorType = MsgBox("Changes made to this _
    customer's details." + vbCrLf + "Do you want to _
    save the changes?", vbYesNo, "WARNING")
    If ErrorType = 6 Then
      cmdSave_Click
    End If
  End If

  Open "AliceFiles\CustomerFile.txt" For Random As _
#1 Len = 360
    Get 1, Update, CustomerDetails
  Close #1
  txtCustID = Update
  txtCustName = CustomerDetails.CustName
  txtCustAddress = CustomerDetails.CustAddress
  txtCustPhone = CustomerDetails.CustPhone
  txtCustEMail = CustomerDetails.CustEmail
  CustChangeFlag = False
End Sub
```

'Check to see if name and address are not empty. Takes
data from the text boxes and puts it in the variable
CustomerDetails then this is saved to the file.

```
Private Sub cmdSave_Click()
  If txtCustName = "" Then
    MsgBox "There is no customer name.", 0, "WARNING"
```

```
        Exit Sub
    End If
    If txtCustAddress = "" Then
      MsgBox "There is no customer address.", 0, _
      "WARNING"
      Exit Sub
    End If
    CustomerDetails.CustName = txtCustName
    CustomerDetails.CustAddress = txtCustAddress
    CustomerDetails.CustPhone = txtCustPhone
    CustomerDetails.CustEmail = txtCustEMail
    Open "AliceFiles\CustomerFile.txt" For Random As _
    #1 Len = 360
      Put 1, CustCurrentRecord, CustomerDetails
    Close #1
    CustChangeFlag = False
  End Sub
```

5 Hard copy of forms

Print the final versions of all of your forms. The only exception to this is if you have a large number of forms and many of them are very similar. In this case, it is sufficient to print out a sample and then to list the other forms used. It is a good idea to show the forms, in use so make sure they contain data before you print them out.

Figure 22.1 FrmCustomerControl

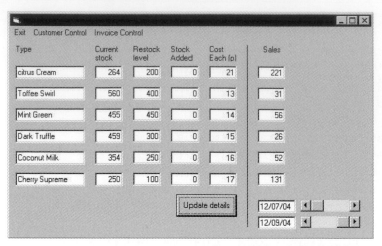

Figure 22.2 FrmStockControl

Evidence for this section is provided by producing the documents and print-outs described above. This also provides evidence of your technical solution, so it is not necessary to print it all out twice.

6 Hard copy of outputs

Evidence for this section is provided by print-out (rather than a screen-grab) of any of the outputs generated by the system and including them either here or in an appendix. In the case of *Alice's Chocolates*, an invoice and a stock control report could be printed.

Example of hardcopy output

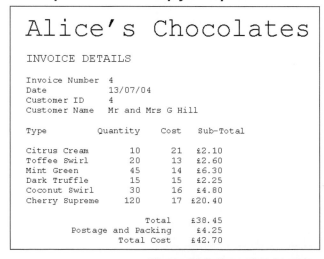

Note: We have had to show a screen-grab here but you must include original hard copies of all outputs from your system.

Figure 22.3 Completed invoice

7 An overview of the system

The easiest way to provide someone else with an overview is through a diagram. You could reproduce the JSP that you produced earlier (Figure 17.2) making sure that it is accurate in relation to the finished program. Alternatively, you could produce a simple hierachy chart showing the main components of the system.

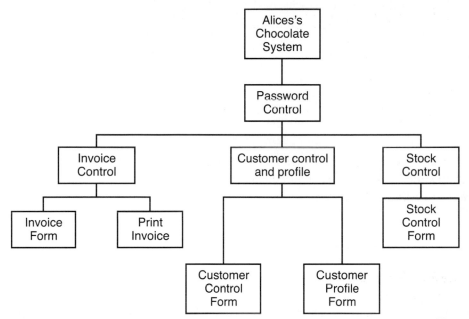

Figure 22.4

 Unit 23 User manual

> The user manual is the guide that you deliver to your user and which tells them how to use the system. It is quite easy to do, but it is also quite time-consuming. You only need to produce a sample of the user guide so you should focus on the core functionality of your program. It is not necessary to produce on-line help within your system, instead you should produce a stand-alone printed document.

Contents

The guide must be written in a style that is appropriate for the user. This means, for example, that if it is an educational game for younger students, the language used in the manual should reflect this. If it is for more technical users, then the manual can be more technical. As a rule, your manual does not have to be very 'wordy'. In essence, it will be a series of bullet-point descriptions describing how to complete a task, followed by appropriate screen-grabs of your system in action.

The manual must be in a separate document and contain the following:

○ A front cover and contents page
○ A brief introduction to the functions of the system
○ Installation instructions
○ A sample of explanations of how to complete tasks, accompanied by screen grabs
○ A sample of error messages and how to recover from them accompanied by screen grabs

Alice's Chocolates — an example

The rest of this unit shows mock-ups of the various sections of the user manual that could be created for the *Alice's Chocolates* system. Please note that these are only samples.

Suggested contents

Introduction
Installation
Section 1: Keeping track of your customers
Section 2: Creating and viewing invoices
Section 3: Keeping track of stock levels
Section 4: Getting your know your customers
Section 5: How to change your password
Error messages and error recovery

Introduction

Welcome to Alice's Chocolate integrated customer database, stock control and invoicing system. This software has been designed to perform a number of tasks.

Please note that you will need a password to enter the system. This is currently set to <ALICE> but we recommend that you change this as soon as you start to enter data into the system. To change the password, see **Section 5** of this guide.

The system has four main sections:

○ **Customer control**: allows you to manage all of your customer's personal details including their name and contact details (see **Section 1**).
○ **Stock control**: allows you to identify the current stock levels of your main products and identifies when stocks are running low (see **Section 2**).
○ **Invoice control**: allows you to create new invoices and examine previous ones (see **Section 3**).
○ **Customer profile**: allows you to analyse the buying patterns of your customers, broken down by all the orders they have ever placed (see **Section 4**).

We recommend that you work through this guide in order. It is essential that you complete the Customer and Stock control details before you attempt to create an invoice.

Installation

The minimum hardware specification for the program is:

○ A Pentium II processor or higher
○ 10Mb of Hard Disk Space
○ 128Mb RAM

To install the program:

○ Insert the CD into your CD drive.
○ Select **My Computer**.
○ Select the CD drive (usually D or E).
○ Double-click on the file **Setup.exe**.
○ Follow the on-screen instructions.

Sample pages

Section 1: Creating a new customer record

When you load the system the first form that is displayed is the **Customer Details** form shown below:

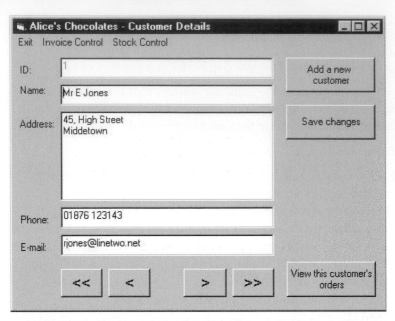

This form allows you to add new customers and change their details. The record currently showing is the first record in the database.

To create a new customer record:

○ Click on the **Add a new customer** button.

All of the details in the text boxes will now be empty apart from the **ID** as shown below. This is because the system automatically allocates a unique number to each new customer.

- ○ Click in the box labelled **Name**.
- ○ Type in the customer's name.
- ○ Complete the address, phone and email details in the same way.
- ○ When complete, click on the **Save changes** button.

Sample error message and how to recover from them

This error occurs when you try to save a new customer record without adding anything to the **Name** field in the **Customer Control** form. Type in the customer name and then click **Save changes**.

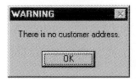

This error occurs when you try to save a new customer record without adding anything to the **Customer address** field in the **Customer Control** form. Type in the customer address and then click **Save changes**.

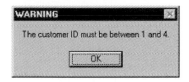

This error occurs if you type an invalid number into the **Customer ID** box in the **Invoice Control** form. You can only type in the number of an existing customer.

⊕ Unit 24 Appraisal

> The appraisal is where you evaluate the success of your project. It is important to be honest in this section and to make use of the feedback that you get from your user.

Matching results to objectives

The start-point is to go back to the objectives that you wrote in the **Analysis** section. Copy and paste them into the **Appraisal** section of your coursework. Now work through each objective in turn, explaining whether you met it or not, how you met it, or why you did not meet it. You do not need to explain in detail how you achieved each objective as you should already have evidence throughout your write-up. You can cross-reference to other sections of your coursework to prove that you have met certain objectives. In particular, much of the evidence is likely to be in the maintenance section.

For example, with *Alices' Chocolates*:

○ To program a fully working solution

I have achieved this objective. I have fully tested my system as can be seen from the testing section on pages # to #. I encountered a number of errors during testing which I have corrected. My user has signed off the system and this can be seen in Appendix 2. It is now in everyday use within the company.

○ To create a printable invoice

I have achieved this objective. An example of a printed invoice can be seen in the **Maintenance** section on page #.

○ To record the number sold, description, price, postage and packing and total cost of an order

I achieved this objective through the invoice control form. I used a control array for the descriptions and prices of each product and then added the postage and packing to this subtotal. The algorithm for this can be seen on page # of my VB code in the **Maintenance** section.

User feedback

The user should have been involved throughout the project and should have just finished testing the system. Therefore, they are in a good position to provide you with feedback. This will need to be in writing. You may choose to prompt your user for comments by asking specific questions about the system and how it meets their objectives. Alternatively, you may ask them to write a letter for you. Either way, you should try to find out what they liked about the system and the things they think could be improved.

It is important that the feedback is honest and objective. You may now want to include criticisms of your solution in your coursework. It is better to include these and indicate how you intend to address the problem, rather than ignoring it. All new systems have problems, so the examiners are expecting to see positive and negative feedback.

The feedback will also help you to identify any possible improvements and extensions and you should include a brief explanation of how you intend to incorporate and suggestions that your user has made.

Your teacher is required to authenticate any user feedback that you put into your coursework. The feedback should be signed and preferably be on headed paper to prove its authenticity. It will be quite obvious if you write the feedback yourself or if you ask one of your friends to do it and this will not be accepted by the exam board.

An example of user feedback is shown below.

15th May 2005

A Student
1 High Street
Anytown
Anyshire

ALICE'S CHOCOLATES

Dear A Student

Thank you very much for producing our new customer database with invoice and stock control. We have been very impressed with the professionalism that you have shown and it was helpful to be involved at the various stages of the project.

As we discussed on the telephone we are happy that most of our objectives have been met. We have a couple of suggestions for how things could be improved and as requested we have some ideas for the next version.

It is fair to say that the new system will save us hours. The customer database aspect meets all of our requirements. It is now very straightforward to add, remove and edit customer details. The invoicing system is also much easier as we are able to retrieve old invoices much more easily than before. The automatic stock control has been the biggest bonus however as this was very time-consuming using the old method.

Alice's Chocolates has always concentrated on making a small range of high quality products. However, we have been thinking about introducing new ranges and the system will have to cope with these as at present we are limited to six items.

We have also had a problem with printing. We bought a new printer and we found that when we print the invoice it prints a second sheet even though the second sheet is blank. This is only a minor annoyance really but I wonder whether this will happen if we try other printers.

However, these are only minor quibbles in what is a major improvement.
Thanks again.

Yours sincerely

Alice Banks
Managing Director

Figure 24.1 User feedback letter

Suggestions for improvements/extensions

The focus of this section should be on ways of improving and extending the system. An improvement might be a way of changing the system to make it better, whereas an extension would involve adding something new to your program.

If you failed to meet some of your objectives, then it would be appropriate to include these in the list of improvements that could be made. In addition to suggesting the improvement, you could also describe in brief how you might incorporate it into the next version. Remember that you are now at the end of the system life cycle so any changes you suggest do not have to implemented.

An example of a further improvement to the *Alice's Chocolates* system might be to extend the number of products that the system can handle, so that rather than being fixed at six, it is infinite. This could be achieved by adding further control arrays to the form. However, if the number of products was to increase beyond around ten, their may not be enough room on the form and a drop-down list might need to be used.

Another improvement could be the addition of an archive system that will remove old invoices from the system, while storing them somewhere just in case they are needed again. This could be achieved by adding a button from the invoice form which opens a new form, where the user is prompted to archive all the existing invoices into a folder and file of their choice.

 Unit 25 Documentation needed for Module 6

At this level, you are expected to create a fully working system. However, you are not required to produce full documentation for every section. In many cases, only a sample of the documentation is needed, as this is enough to prove that you have certain skills. We have indicated in each of the units in this section where a sample is required.

The purpose of this unit is to summarise the documentation required at this level, providing what is effectively a checklist. It does not aim to explain the detail of what should be in each section, as this has already been covered in Units 16 to 24 and has been cross-referenced here.

How much to write

Most exam boards put a guideline of somewhere around 4000 words, which is approximately ten pages of typed A4 (assuming Times New Roman, size 12). AQA removed the 4000 word limit in 2005. This seems quite low, given the amount needed in some sections. In addition to this, you will have a print-out your VB code and screen grabs of your system, which may run to several pages. In reality, most A2 projects run somewhere between 50 and 100 pages in total. You should try to avoid including unnecessary duplication, but you also need to do justice to yourself and include evidence of everything you have done.

Analysis

- Background information and description of the problems should be written in continuous prose. Do not talk about the solution at all at this stage — just the problem.
- Name the user or users and other relevant information about them, for example, their job title. You could explain their level of competence, as this will have a direct bearing on the system that you design.
- Full feasibility study including a justification of the final solution.
- Data Flow Diagrams for the existing and proposed system
- Objectives and limitations of the project

Design

See Units 17 to 19 for examples of what to include. Covers:

Overall system design

- System flowchart
- Structure diagram
- Modular structure
- List of suitable algorithms

Definition of data requirements and validation

- List of record and data structures
- List of files explaining how they are organised and processed
- List of variables and constants
- Explanation of data entry and validation
- Explanation of the security and integrity of data
- A test strategy

User interface design

- Sample of form designs
- Sample of printed output designs

Technical solution

The marks awarded in this section are for creating a working system that meets the design. The exam board do not want your system supplied on disk. They need a hardcopy of your code. The evidence needed here is the same as that required in the **System Maintenance** section so there is no need to duplicate here.

You should also include examples of the solution in use.

System testing

- A test strategy, including an explanation of the test data which should include valid, invalid and extreme data
- Test tables showing expected and actual results
- Selected hardcopy to prove that testing has been carried out, cross-referenced to the test table

System maintenance

○ Hardcopy of your VB code, which should be commented within VB.
○ Samples of form designs (there is no need to include every form, particularly if you have several which perform a similar function)
○ Details of procedures and their purpose
○ Details of variables and their purpose

User manual

A separate document must be produced which should include:

○ A brief introduction to your program
○ Installation instructions
○ Details of the processes your system can carry out
○ Samples of screen grabs with live data and instructions of how to use the system
○ Samples of error messages and how to correct the errors

Appraisal

○ Go through each of the objectives in turn, with a paragraph explaining how you met each one
○ You need around six detailed suggestion, for how you could improve or extend the solution
○ You should include feedback from your user in the form of a letter or questionnaire.

Quality of communication

Marks are available for the way in which you present your work and your use of grammar, punctuation and spelling. Make sure that your work is clearly and logically presented, including a contents page and page numbering. Check your spelling and grammar and make sure that you have used technical terms appropriately and correctly. You should use the headings AQA suggest and your project should be arranged in that order.

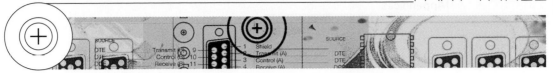

PART THREE

Appendices

⊕ Appendix 1 Code listing and forms for Part 1 projects

Unit 2 Text editor

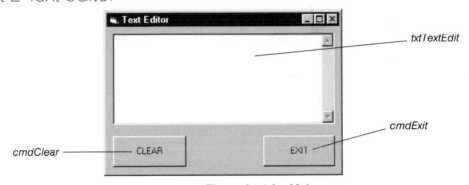

Figure A1.1 frmMainpage

```
Private Sub cmdClear_Click()
  txtTextEdit.Text = ""
End Sub
```

```
Private Sub cmdExit_Click()
  Unload Me
  End
End Sub
```

Unit 3 Basic calculator

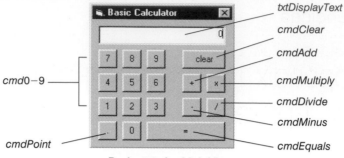

Project 2: frmMainView

```
Option Explicit
Dim FirstNumber As Single
Dim SecondNumber As Single
Dim AnswerNumber As Single
Dim ArithmeticProcess As String
```

```
'The next 10 procedures deal with clicks on numeric keys
Private Sub cmd0_Click()
  txtDisplay.Text = txtDisplay.Text + "0"
End Sub
```

```
Private Sub cmd1_Click()
  txtDisplay.Text = txtDisplay.Text + "1"
End Sub
```

```
Private Sub cmd2_Click()
  txtDisplay.Text = txtDisplay.Text + "2"
End Sub
```

```
Private Sub cmd3_Click()
  txtDisplay.Text = txtDisplay.Text + "3"
End Sub
```

```
Private Sub cmd4_Click()
  txtDisplay.Text = txtDisplay.Text + "4"
End Sub
```

```
Private Sub cmd5_Click()
  txtDisplay.Text = txtDisplay.Text + "5"
End Sub

Private Sub cmd6_Click()
  txtDisplay.Text = txtDisplay.Text + "6"
End Sub

Private Sub cmd7_Click()
  txtDisplay.Text = txtDisplay.Text + "7"
End Sub

Private Sub cmd8_Click()
  txtDisplay.Text = txtDisplay.Text + "8"
End Sub

Private Sub cmd9_Click()
  txtDisplay.Text = txtDisplay.Text + "9"
End Sub

Private Sub cmdPoint_Click()
  txtDisplay.Text = txtDisplay.Text + "."
End Sub

' reset the text display
Private Sub cmdClear_Click()
  txtDisplay.Text = "0"
End Sub

Private Sub cmdAdd_Click()
  FirstNumber = Val(txtDisplay.Text)
  txtDisplay.Text = "0"
  ArithmeticProcess = "+"
End Sub

Private Sub cmdDivide_Click()
  FirstNumber = Val(txtDisplay.Text)
  txtDisplay.Text = "0"
  ArithmeticProcess = "/"
End Sub
```

```vb
Private Sub cmdMultiply_Click()
  FirstNumber = Val(txtDisplay.Text)
  txtDisplay.Text = "0"
  ArithmeticProcess = "x"
End Sub


Private Sub cmdSubtract_Click()
  FirstNumber = Val(txtDisplay.Text)
  txtDisplay.Text = "0"
  ArithmeticProcess = "-"
End Sub


Private Sub cmdEquals_Click()

  SecondNumber = Val(txtDisplay.Text)

  If ArithmeticProcess = "+" Then
    AnswerNumber = FirstNumber + SecondNumber
  End If

  If ArithmeticProcess = "-" Then
    AnswerNumber = FirstNumber - SecondNumber
  End If

  If ArithmeticProcess = "x" Then
    AnswerNumber = FirstNumber * SecondNumber
  End If

  If ArithmeticProcess = "/" Then
    If SecondNumber = 0 Then
      MsgBox "You cannot divide by zero.", 0, "WARNING"
      Exit Sub
    End If
    AnswerNumber = FirstNumber / SecondNumber
  End If

  txtDisplay.Text = AnswerNumber

End Sub
```

Unit 4 Car Hire

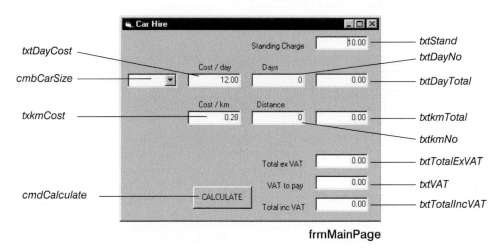

frmMainPage

```
Private Sub cmbCarSize_Click()
   If cmbCarSize.Text = "Small" Then
     txtDayCost.Text = "12.00"
   End If
   If cmbCarSize.Text = "Medium" Then
     txtDayCost.Text = "15.00"
   End If
   If cmbCarSize.Text = "Large" Then
     txtDayCost.Text = "21.00"
   End If
End Sub
```

```
Private Sub cmdCalculate_Click()

   txtDayTotal = Val(txtDayCost) * Val(txtDayNo)
   txtkmTotal = Val(txtKMCost) * Val(txtKMNo.Text)
   txtTotalexVAT = Format(Val(txtDayTotal) + _
   Val(txtkmTotal) + Val(txtStand), "#.00")
   txtVAT = 0.175 * Val(txtTotalexVAT)
   txtTotalincVAT = Format(Val(txtTotalexVAT) + _
Val(txtVAT), "##.00")

End Sub
```

Unit 5 Invoice Creator

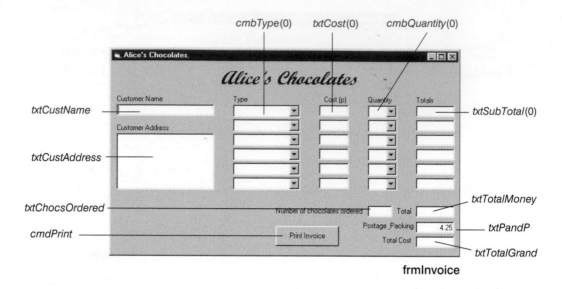

cmbType(0)   txtCost(0)   cmbQuantity(0)

txtCustName

txtCustAddress

txtChocsOrdered

cmdPrint

txtSubTotal(0)

txtTotalMoney

txtPandP

txtTotalGrand

frmInvoice

```vb
Option Explicit
Dim MoneyCounter As Single
Dim ChocCounter As Integer
Dim Counter As Integer
```

```vb
Private Sub cmbType_Click(Index As Integer)

  ' change the price dependant on the type
  Select Case cmbType(Index)
    Case "Citrus Cream": txtCost(Index) = "65"
    Case "Toffee Swirl": txtCost(Index) = "54"
    Case "Mint Green": txtCost(Index) = "37"
    Case "Dark Truffle": txtCost(Index) = "43"
    Case "Coconut Milk": txtCost(Index) = "76"
    Case "Cherry Supreme": txtCost(Index) = "98"
    Case Else: txtCost(Index) = ""
  End Select

  ' calculate the total cost for chosen type
  txtSubTotal(Index) = Format(Val(txtCost(Index)) * _
      Val(cmbQuantity(Index)) / 100, "0.00")
```

```
' add up the subtotals for each of the types
MoneyCounter = 0
For Counter = 0 To 5
  MoneyCounter = MoneyCounter + _
  Val(txtSubTotal(Counter))
Next

' display the total owed and add on P&P
txtTotalMoney = MoneyCounter
txtTotalGrand = Val(txtPandP) + Val(txtTotalMoney)

' find the total number of chocolates being ordered
ChocCounter = 0
For Counter = 0 To 5
  ChocCounter = ChocCounter + Val(cmbQuantity(Counter))
Next
txtChocsOrdered = Val(ChocCounter)

End Sub
```

```
Private Sub cmbQuantity_Click(Index As Integer)
  ' this procedure invoked when the quantity is changed
  ' this then forces the row calculations be recalculated
  Call cmbType_Click(Index)
End Sub
```

```
Private Sub cmdPrint_Click()
  cmdPrint.Visible = False
  frmInvoice.PrintForm
  cmdPrint.Visible = True
End Sub
```

Unit 7 Jack's Garage

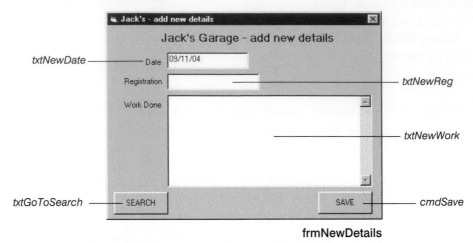

txtNewDate — Date [09/11/04]

Registration [ ] — *txtNewReg*

Work Done [ ] — *txtNewWork*

txtGoToSearch — [SEARCH] [SAVE] — *cmdSave*

frmNewDetails

```
Private Sub Form_Load()
  txtNewDate = Date
End Sub
```

```
Private Sub cmdGoToSearch_Click()
  frmSearch.Show
  frmNewDetails.Hide
End Sub
```

```
Private Sub cmdSave_Click()

  If txtNewDate = "" Then
    MsgBox "You must enter a date", 0, "Error"
    Exit Sub
  End If

  If txtNewReg = "" Then
    MsgBox "You must enter a registration number", 0, _
      "Error"
    Exit Sub
  End If

  If txtNewWork = "" Then
    MsgBox "You must enter details of the work carried _
      out", 0, "Error"
    Exit Sub
  End If
```

```
Open "CarHistory.txt" For Append As #1
   Print #1, txtNewDate
   Print #1, txtNewReg
   Print #1, txtNewWork
Close #1

txtNewReg = ""
txtNewWork = ""

End Sub
```

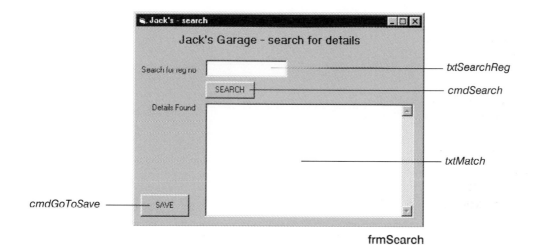

frmSearch

```
Option Explicit
Dim inputDate As String
Dim inputRegNo As String
Dim inputText As String
```

```
Private Sub cmdGoToSave_Click()
   frmSearch.Hide
   frmNewDetails.Show
End Sub
```

```
Private Sub cmdSearch_Click()
  txtMatch = ""
  Open "CarHistory.txt" For Input As #1
    Do
      Input #1, inputDate
      Input #1, inputRegNo
      Input #1, inputText
      If inputRegNo = txtSearchReg Then
        txtMatch = txtMatch + inputDate + vbCrLf + _
        inputText + vbCrLf
      End If
    Loop Until EOF(1)
  Close #1
End Sub
```

Unit 8 Alice's Chocolates

Code from Module 1

```
' defines a user defined type that will be available
' throughout the project

Public RecordCount As Integer

Type RecordDetails
  RecordType As String * 14
  RecordCurrent As Integer
  RecordRestock As Integer
End Type
```

frmMenu

```
Private Sub cmdAddSales_Click()
  frmMenu.Hide
  frmUpdateRecords.Show
End Sub
```

```
Private Sub cmdCurrentStock_Click()
  frmMenu.Hide
  frmViewRecords.Show
End Sub
```

```
Private Sub cmdRestock_Click()
  frmMenu.Hide
  frmAlterRecords.Show
End Sub
```

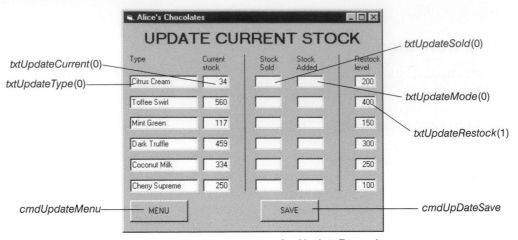

frmUpdateRecords

```
Private UpdateRecord As RecordDetails

Private Sub cmdUpDateMenu_Click()
  Unload frmUpdateRecords
  frmMenu.Show
End Sub

Private Sub Form_Load()

  ' upload data to screeen
  Open "ChocFile.txt" For Random As #1 Len = 18
    For Counter = 1 To 6
      Get 1, Counter, UpdateRecord
      txtUpDateType (Counter - 1) = UpdateRecord. _
      RecordType
      txtUpDateCurrent (Counter - 1) = UpdateRecord. _
      RecordCurrent
      txtUpDateRestock (Counter - 1) = UpdateRecord. _
      RecordRestock
    Next
Close #1

End Sub

Private Sub cmdUpDateSave_Click()

  ' confirm the save
  ErrorType = MsgBox ("Are you sure you want to save?", _
  vbYesNo + vbDefaultButton2, "WARNING")
  If ErrorType = 7 Then
    Exit Sub
  End If
```

```
Open "ChocFile.txt" For Random As #1 Len = 18

  ' calculate new stock levels
  For RecordCount = 1 To 6
    txtUpDateCurrent (RecordCount - 1) = _
    Val(txtUpDateCurrent (RecordCount - 1)) + _
    Val(txtUpdateMade (RecordCount - 1)) - _
    Val(txtUpDateSold(RecordCount - 1))
    txtUpDateSold(RecordCount - 1) = ""
    txtUpdateMade(RecordCount - 1) = ""
  Next

  ' save details to file
  For RecordCount = 1 To 6
    UpdateRecord.RecordType = txtUpDateType _
    (RecordCount - 1)
    UpdateRecord.RecordCurrent = Val(txtUpDateCurrent _
    (RecordCount - 1))
    UpdateRecord.RecordRestock = Val(txtUpDateRestock _
    (RecordCount - 1))
    Put 1, RecordCount, UpdateRecord
  Next

Close #1

  ' check for low stock levels
  ErrorMessage = ""
  For RecordCount = 1 To 6
    If Val(txtUpDateCurrent(RecordCount - 1)) < _
    Val(txtUpDateRestock(RecordCount - 1)) Then
      ErrorMessage = ErrorMessage + txtUpDateType _
      (RecorfdCount - 1) + vbCrLf
    End If
  Next
  If ErrorMessage <>"" Then
    MsgBox "You need to restock the following _
    chocolates" + vbCrLf + errorMessage, vbCritical, _
    "WARNING"
  End If

End Sub
```

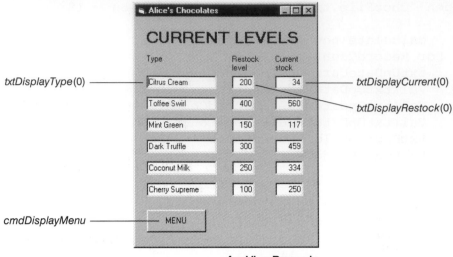

txtDisplayType(0)   *txtDisplayCurrent*(0)

txtDisplayRestock(0)

cmdDisplayMenu

frmViewRecords

```
Private DisplayRecord As RecordDetails
```

```
Private Sub cmdDisplayMenu_Click()
  Unload frmViewRecords
  frmMenu.Show
End Sub
```

```
Private Sub Form_Load()

  Open "ChocFile.txt" For Random As #1 Len = 18
    For Counter = 1 To 6
      Get 1, Counter, DisplayRecord
      txtDisplayType(Counter - 1) = _
      DisplayRecord.RecordType
      txtDisplayCurrent(Counter - 1) =  _
      DisplayRecord.RecordCurrent
      txtDisplayRestock(Counter - 1) =  _
      DisplayRecord.RecordRestock
    Next
  Close #1

End Sub
```

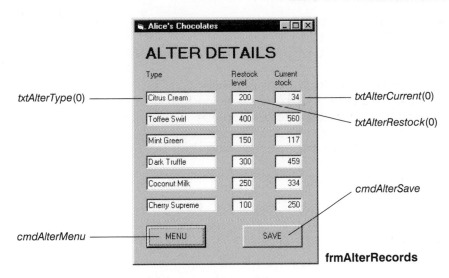

txtAlterType(0)			txtAlterCurrent(0)
			txtAlterRestock(0)
			cmdAlterSave
cmdAlterMenu			

frmAlterRecords

```
Private SaveRecord As RecordDetails

Private Sub Form_Load()

  Open "ChocFile.txt" For Random As #1 Len = 18
    For RecordCount = 1 To 6
      Get 1, RecordCount, SaveRecord
      txtAlterType(RecordCount - 1) = _
      SaveRecord.RecordType
      txtAlterCurrent(RecordCount - 1) = _
      SaveRecord.RecordCurrent
      txtAlterRestock(RecordCount - 1) = _
      SaveRecord.RecordRestock
    Next
  Close #1

End Sub

Private Sub cmdAlterMenu_Click()
  frmAlterRecords.unload
  frmMenu.Show
End Sub

Private Sub cmdAlterSave_Click()

  ErrorType = MsgBox("Are you sure you want to save?", _
  vbYesNo + vbDefaultButton2, "WARNING")
  If ErrorType = 7 Then
    Exit Sub
  End If
```

```
Open "ChocFile.txt" For Random As #1 Len = 18
   For RecordCount = 1 To 6
     SaveRecord.RecordType = txtAlterType(RecordCount _
- 1)
     SaveRecord.RecordCurrent = _
     Val(txtAlterCurrent(RecordCount - 1))
     SaveRecord.RecordRestock = _
     Val(txtAlterRestock(RecordCount - 1))
     Put 1, RecordCount, SaveRecord
   Next
 Close #1

End Sub
```

Units 9 and 10 Chris' Car Customiser

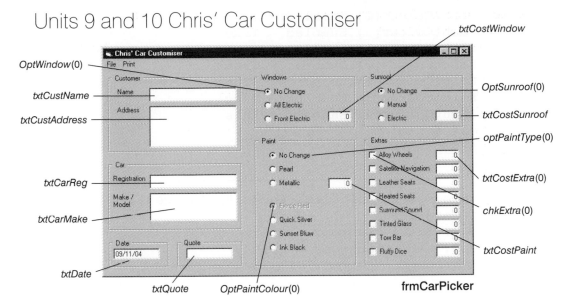

txtCostWindow

OptWindow(0)

txtCustName

txtCustAddress

txtCarReg

txtCarMake

txtDate

txtQuote

OptPaintColour(0)

OptSunroof(0)

txtCostSunroof

optPaintType(0)

txtCostExtra(0)

chkExtra(0)

txtCostPaint

frmCarPicker

Unit 9

```
'ThisDir is declared as a public variable so it will be
'available through the whole form. It will store the
'pathname for the root folder
Public ThisDir As String
```

```
Private Sub Form_Load()
  txtDate = Date
  ThisDir = CurDir + "\Car Quotes\"
End Sub
```

```
Private Sub optPaintType_Click(Index As Integer)
  Select Case Index
  Case 0: txtCostPaint = "0"
    optPaintColour(0).Enabled = False
    optPaintColour(1).Enabled = False
    optPaintColour(2).Enabled = False
    optPaintColour(3).Enabled = False
  Case 1: txtCostPaint = "600"
    If optPaintColour(1).Value = True Then
      MsgBox "Pearl paint is not available in Quick _
      Silver.", 16, "WARNING"
      optPaintColour(1).Value = False
    End If
    optPaintColour(0).Enabled = True
    optPaintColour(1).Enabled = False
```

```
      optPaintColour(2).Enabled = True
      optPaintColour(3).Enabled = True
    Case 2: txtCostPaint = "720"
      optPaintColour(0).Enabled = True
      optPaintColour(1).Enabled = True
      optPaintColour(2).Enabled = True
      optPaintColour(3).Enabled = False
  End Select
  Call AddUp
End Sub


Private Sub optSunroof_Click(Index As Integer)
  Select Case Index
    Case 0: txtCostSunroof = "0"
    Case 2: txtCostSunroof = "300"
    Case 1: txtCostSunroof = "560"
  End Select
  Call AddUp
End Sub


Private Sub optWindow_Click(Index As Integer)
  Select Case Index
    Case 0: txtCostWindow = "0"
    Case 1: txtCostWindow = "450"
    Case 2: txtCostWindow = "250"
  End Select
  Call AddUp
End Sub


Private Sub chkExtra_Click(Index As Integer)

  For Counter = 0 To 7
    txtCostExtra(Counter) = 0
  Next

  If chkExtra(0).Value = 1 Then txtCostExtra(0) = "280"
  If chkExtra(1).Value = 1 Then txtCostExtra(1) = "120"
  If chkExtra(2).Value = 1 Then txtCostExtra(2) = "200"
  If chkExtra(3).Value = 1 Then txtCostExtra(3) = "100"
  If chkExtra(4).Value = 1 Then txtCostExtra(4) = "60"
  If chkExtra(5).Value = 1 Then txtCostExtra(5) = "240"
  If chkExtra(6).Value = 1 Then txtCostExtra(6) = "180"
  If chkExtra(7).Value = 1 Then txtCostExtra(7) = "5"

  Call AddUp

End Sub
```

```
Private Sub AddUp()

    txtQuote = Val(txtCostWindow) + Val(txtCostSunroof) _
    + Val(txtCostPaint)
    For Counter = 0 To 7
        txtQuote = Val(txtQuote) + Val(txtCostExtra(Counter))
    Next

End Sub
```

```
Private Sub mnuSave_Click()

    Open ThisDir + txtCarReg + ".cqu" For Output As #1
        Print #1, txtDate
        Print #1, txtCustName
        Print #1, txtCustAddress
        Print #1, "AddressEnd"
        Print #1, txtCarReg
        Print #1, txtCarMake
        For Counter = 0 To 2
            If optWindow(Counter) = True Then Print #1, Counter
        Next
        For Counter = 0 To 2
            If optSunroof(Counter) = True Then Print #1, _
            Counter
        Next
        For Counter = 0 To 2
            If optPaintType(Counter) = True Then Print #1, _
            Counter
        Next
        For Counter = 0 To 3
            If optPaintColour(Counter) = True Then Print #1, _
            Counter
        Next
        For Counter = 0 To 7
            Print #1, chkExtra(Counter)
        Next
        Close #1
End Sub
```

Code for Unit 10

```
Private Sub mnuLoad_Click()

'look in the folder for files with e extension cqu
On Error GoTo traperror
cdlFile.Filter = ".cqu"
  cdlFile.ShowOpen
  Open cdlFile.filename For Input As #1

    Line Input #1, Temp: txtDate = Temp
    Line Input #1, Temp: txtCustName = Temp

    txtCustAddress = ""
    Temp = ""
    Do
      If Temp <> "" Then txtCustAddress = _
      txtCustAddress + Temp + vbCrLf
      Line Input #1, Temp
    Loop Until Temp = "AddressEnd"

    Input #1, Temp: txtCarReg = Temp
    Input #1, Temp: txtCarMake = Temp

    Input #1, TempOpt: optWindow(TempOpt).Value = True
    Input #1, TempOpt: optSunroof(TempOpt).Value = True
    Input #1, TempOpt: optPaintType(TempOpt).Value = True
    Input #1, TempOpt: optPaintColour(TempOpt).Value = _
      True
    For Counter = 0 To 7
      Input #1, TempOpt: chkExtra(Counter) = TempOpt
    Next

  Close #1
  Exit Sub

traperror:
End Sub
```

```
Private Sub mnuCheck_Click()

'this procedure checks for all the quotes that are
'more than 30 days old
Dim TempDate As Date

   CheckFile = Dir(ThisDir, vbNormal)
   Do While CheckFile <> ""
   If Right(CheckFile, 3) = "cqu" Then

   Open CurDir + "\Car Quotes\" + CheckFile For _
       Input As #1
       Line Input #1, TempDate
       If Date - TempDate > 30 Then
         txtDate = TempDate
         Line Input #1, Temp: txtCustName = Temp
         txtCustAddress = ""
         Temp = ""
         Do
           If Temp <> "" Then txtCustAddress = _
           txtCustAddress + Temp + vbCrLf
           Line Input #1, Temp
         Loop Until Temp = "AddressEnd"
         Input #1, Temp: txtCarReg = Temp
         Input #1, Temp: txtCarMake = Temp
         Input #1, TempOpt: optWindow(TempOpt).Value = True
         Input #1, TempOpt: optSunroof(TempOpt).Value = True
         Input #1, TempOpt: optPaintType(TempOpt).Value = True
         Input #1, TempOpt: optPaintColour(TempOpt).Value = True
         For Counter = 0 To 7
           Input #1, TempOpt: chkExtra(Counter) = TempOpt
         Next
         Close #1
         ErrorType = MsgBox("This quote is more than 30 _
         days old." + vbCrLf + "Do you want to delete _
         it?", vbYesNo + vbDefaultButton2, "Check Quote")
         If ErrorType = 6 Then
           Kill ThisDir + CheckFile
         End If
       Else
         Close #1
       End If
     End If
   CheckFile = Dir
   Loop
End Sub
```

```
Private Sub mnuPrint_Click()

    cdlPrint.ShowPrinter
    On Error GoTo traperror

    Printer.FontName = "Times New Roman"
    Printer.FontBold = True
    Printer.FontSize = 18
    Printer.Print "Chris's Car Quotation"
    Printer.Print
    Printer.FontName = "Courier New"
    Printer.FontBold = False
    Printer.FontSize = 12
    Printer.Print "Date"; Tab; txtDate
    Printer.Print "Name"; Tab; txtCustName
    Printer.Print "Car reg"; Tab; txtCarReg
    Printer.Print "Car type"; Tab; txtCarMake
    Printer.Print

    Printer.Print "Windows - ";
    If optWindow(0).Value = True Then Printer.Print "no _
        change";
    If optWindow(1).Value = True Then Printer.Print _
        "front electric";
    If optWindow(2).Value = True Then Printer.Print "all _
        electric";
    Printer.Print Tab; txtCostWindow

    Printer.Print "Paint Type - ";
    If optPaintType(0).Value = True Then Printer.Print _
        "no change";
    If optPaintType(1).Value = True Then Printer.Print _
        "pearl";
    If optPaintType(2).Value = True Then Printer.Print _
        "metallic";
    Printer.Print Tab; txtCostPaint

    If optPaintType(0).Value = False Then _
      Printer.Print "Paint colour - ";
      If optPaintColour(0).Value = True Then _
        Printer.Print "fierce red"
      If optPaintColour(1).Value = True Then _
        Printer.Print "quick silver"
```

```
      If optPaintColour(2).Value = True Then _
         Printer.Print "sunset blue"
      If optPaintColour(3).Value = True Then _
         Printer.Print "ink black"
   End If

   Printer.Print "Sunroof - ";
   If optSunroof(0).Value = True Then Printer.Print "no _
         change";
   If optSunroof(1).Value = True Then Printer.Print _
         "manual";
   If optSunroof(2).Value = True Then Printer.Print _
         "electric";
   Printer.Print Tab; txtCostSunroof
   Printer.Print

   For Counter = 0 To 7
   If chkExtra(Counter).Value = 1 Then
   Printer.Print Left(chkExtra(Counter).Caption, 12);
   Printer.Print Tab; txtCostExtra(Counter)
   End If
   Next

   Printer.Print
   Printer.Print "Total"; Tab; txtQuote

   Printer.EndDoc
   Exit Sub

traperror:
End Sub
```

Unit 11 The Fruit Selector

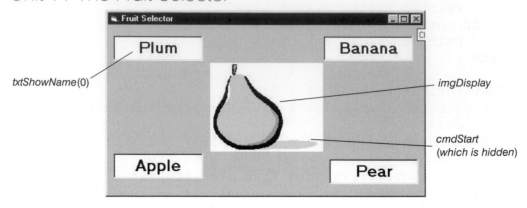

txtShowName(0)

imgDisplay

cmdStart
(which is hidden)

```
Option Explicit

Dim ImageName() As String
Dim CheckFile As String
Dim ChosenFruit As Integer
Dim Counter As Integer
Dim ImageCounter As Integer
Dim ThisDir As String
```

```
Private Sub Form_Load()

  Randomize
  ThisDir = CurDir

  'count the number of the files in the image folder
  ImageCounter = 0
  CheckFile = Dir(ThisDir + "\ImageFolder\", _
  vbDirectory)
  Do While CheckFile <> ""
   If LCase(Right(CheckFile, 3)) = "bmp" Then
     ImageCounter = ImageCounter + 1
   End If
   CheckFile = Dir
  Loop

  ReDim ImageName(ImageCounter)

  'load the file names into the array ImageName
  Counter = 0
  CheckFile = Dir(ThisDir + "\ImageFolder\", vbDirectory)
  Do While CheckFile <> ""
    If LCase(Right(CheckFile, 3)) = "bmp" Then
      Counter = Counter + 1
```

```
        ImageName(Counter) = Left(CheckFile, _
        Len(CheckFile) - 4)
      End If
      CheckFile = Dir
    Loop

End Sub
```

```
Private Sub cmdStart_Click()

  'select an image from the array
  ChosenFruit = Int(ImageCounter * Rnd() + 1)
  imgDisplay.Picture = LoadPicture(ThisDir + _
  "\ImageFolder\" + ImageName(ChosenFruit) + ".bmp")

  'load four image names on to the screen
  For Counter = 0 To 3
    txtShowName(Counter) = ImageName(Int(ImageCounter _
    * Rnd() + 1))
  Next

  'make sure the actual name is on display
  txtShowName(Int(4 * Rnd())) = ImageName(ChosenFruit)
  cmdStart.Visible = False

End Sub
```

```
Private Sub txtShowName_Click(Index As Integer)

  If txtShowName(Index) = ImageName(ChosenFruit) Then
    imgDisplay.Picture = LoadPicture("tick.bmp")
  Else
    lblWrong.Visible = True
    lblWrong.Caption = "The answer was " + _
    ImageName(ChosenFruit)
  End If

  Timer.Enabled = True

End Sub
```

```
Private Sub Timer_Timer()

  Timer.Enabled = False
  lblWrong.Caption = ""
  cmdStart_Click

End Sub
```

Unit 12 The Video Hire Shop

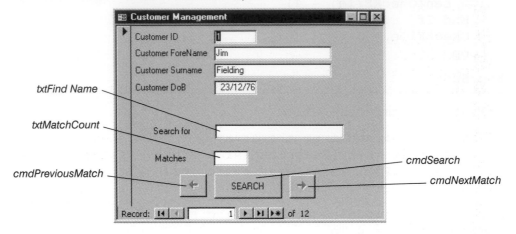

```
Option Compare Database

Dim CountFind As Integer
Dim ThisMatch As Integer
```

```
Private Sub cmdSearch_Click()

  cmdPreviousMatch.Enabled = False
  cmdNextMatch.Enabled = False

  'check for something to search for
  If IsNull(txtFindName) = True Then
    MsgBox "There is nothing to search for.", 0, _
    "Search Failed"
    Exit Sub
  End If

  Customer_ForeName.SetFocus
  DoCmd.FindRecord txtFindName

  'no matching records
  If Customer_ForeName <> txtFindName Then
    MsgBox "Failed to find any matching records.", 0, _
    "Search Failed"
  txtFindName.SetFocus
  Exit Sub
  End If
```

```
'count number of matching records
CountFind = 0
Do
  CurrentCustomer_ID = Customer_ID
  DoCmd.FindRecord txtFindName, , , , , False
  CountFind = CountFind + 1
Loop Until CurrentCustomer_ID = Customer_ID

ThisMatch = CountFind
txtMatchCount = ThisMatch & " / " & CountFind
If CountFind > 1 Then cmdPreviousMatch.Enabled = True

End Sub
```

```
Private Sub cmdPreviousMatch_Click()

  'move back a matching record
  Customer_ForeName.SetFocus
  DoCmd.FindRecord txtFindName, , , acUp, , , False
  cmdNextMatch.Enabled = True
  ThisMatch = ThisMatch - 1
  If ThisMatch = 1 Then cmdPreviousMatch.Enabled = False
  txtMatchCount = ThisMatch & " / " & CountFind

End Sub
```

```
Private Sub cmdNextMatch_Click()

  'move on to the next matching record
  Customer_ForeName.SetFocus
  DoCmd.FindRecord txtFindName, , , acDown, , , False
  cmdPreviousMatch.Enabled = True
  ThisMatch = ThisMatch + 1
  If ThisMatch = CountFind Then cmdNextMatch.Enabled = _
  False
  txtMatchCount = ThisMatch & " / " & CountFind
End Sub
```

Unit 13 Alice's Chocolates stock control system

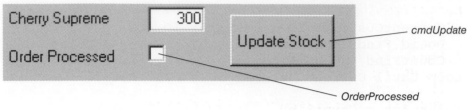

```
Option Compare Database

Private Sub cmdUpdate_Click()

  'check to see if the order has already been processed
  If [order processed] = True Then
    MsgBox "This order has already been processed.", _
0, "WARNING"
    Exit Sub
  End If

  'open the stock form. Find the first and last records
  LowStock = ""
  DoCmd.OpenForm "frmStock"
  Forms!frmstock.Recordset.MoveLast
  LastName = Forms!frmstock.ChocType
  Forms!frmstock.Recordset.MoveFirst

  'check to see if there is sufficient stock
  Do
    ThisName = Forms!frmstock.ChocType
    If Forms!frmOrder!(ThisName) > _
    Forms!frmstock!Current Stock Level Then LowStock = _
    LowStock + vbCrLf + ThisName
    Forms!frmstock.Recordset.MoveNext
  Loop Until ThisName = LastName
  DoCmd.Close

  If LowStock <> "" Then
    MsgBox "Unable to process order - stocks of the _
    following" + vbCrLf + "chocolate(s) are too low to _
    meet this order" + vbCrLf + vbrclf + LowStock, 0, _
    "WARNING"
    Exit Sub
  End If
```

```
'enough stock so deduct this order
DoCmd.OpenForm "frmStock"
Forms!frmstock.Recordset.MoveFirst
Do
   ThisName = Forms!frmstock.ChocType
   Forms!frmstock!Current Stock Level = _
   Forms!frmstock!Current Stock Level - Forms!frmOrder! _
   (ThisName)
   Forms!frmstock.Recordset.MoveNext
Loop Until ThisName = LastName

DoCmd.Close

Forms!frmOrder![order processed] = True

'check to see if any of stock levels are too low
ReStock = ""
DoCmd.OpenForm "frmStock"
Forms!frmstock.Recordset.MoveFirst

Do
   ThisName = Forms!frmstock.ChocType
   If Forms!frmstock!Current Stock Level < _
   Forms!frmstock!ReStock_Level Then ReStock = ReStock _
   + vbCrLf + ThisName
   Forms!frmstock.Recordset.MoveNext
Loop Until ThisName = LastName

DoCmd.Close

If ReStock <> "" Then
   MsgBox "The following chocolate(s) need re- _
   stocking." + vbCrLf + vbrclf + ReStock, 0, "WARNING"
   Exit Sub
End If

End Sub
```

⊕ Appendix 2 — Control name prefixes

Using specific prefixes for the names of controls makes them easier to identify when you are creating code. These are the prefixes recommended by Microsoft.

chk	Check Box
cdl	Common Dialog Box
cmb	Combo Box
cmd	Command Button
dir	Directory List Box
drv	Drive List Box
flb	File List Box
fra	Frame
frm	Form
hsb	Horizontal Scroll Bar
img	Image
lbl	Label
lst	List Box
mnu	Menu
opt	Option Button
pic	Picture Box
tmr	Timer
txt	Text Box
vsb	Vertical Scroll Bar

⊕ Appendix 3 — Message boxes

Once a message boxes has been displayed, the user cannot carry on with the rest of the program until they have clicked on one of the options offered by the message box.

You can use a message box to force the user to decide whether or not a save operation should go ahead, or you might use one to make sure the user is aware of the conditions attached to using some software.

Message boxes have two formats.

The first just gives information. It cannot respond to user input. The general syntax is:

```
MsgBox "Put paper in the printer then click 'ok'" , _
0 , "Take Care"
```

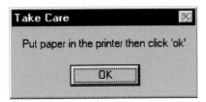

Figure A3.1

The second type returns a value that is linked to the type of warning message you have chosen to display and the particular button the user has clicked. The general syntax is:

```
ButtonPressed = MsgBox ("Text in here", _
ActionNumber , "Title text")
```

The value that `ActionNumber` takes dictates what options the user is given. `ActionNumber` is made up of one number from each of the following tables:

0	Ignore		0	No icon		0	Default button 1
1	OK/Cancel		16	Critical Icon		256	Default button 2
2	Abort/Retry/Ignore		32	Warning Query		512	Default button 3
3	Yes/No/Cancel		48	Warning Message		768	Default button 4
4	Yes/No		64	Information Message			
5	Retry/Cancel						

A message box that gives the user the option of clicking on **Yes** or **No**, displays a warning symbol and makes the default option the second button in the list – in this case **No**, would have an `ActionNumber` of 4 + 48 + 256 = 308.

```
ButtonPressed = MsgBox "Do you want to _
continue?",308,"WARNING"
```

would create:

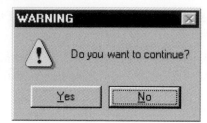

Figure A3.2

Once the user has clicked on one of the options, the message box returns a value which identifies which button has been pressed. In this example, this is assigned to the variable `ButtonPressed`.

1	OK
2	Cancel
3	Abort
4	Retry
5	Ignore
6	Yes
7	No

In this example clicking on the **No** button would return the value 7. The user can then make use of this value when they decide what to make the program do next.

Appendix 4 — DoCmd FindRecord parameters in VBA

DoCmd is a very powerful command and it supports many methods. One of the most useful is the ability to search through the records in a dataset. The command `DoCmd FindRecord` is followed by up to seven parameters. The default values in all but the first of these will be assumed if the value is left blank.

`Findwhat`	The text, number or date you are searching for. You can, of course, use a variable in here.
`Match`	Where to look for the search item: ○ `acAnywhere` will look for the search item within the attribute so it would find **stop** in **Christoper**. ○ `acEntire` will only return a match if the entire search matches so it would not find **Ann** in **Anne** ○ `acStart` looks for the search word at the start of the attribute. The default setting is `acEntire`.
`Matchcase`	The search will be case sensitive if you set this parameter to `True`. The default is `False`.
`Search direction`	This can be set to: ○ `acDown` forces the search to move on through the records for the point you start from. ○ `acSearchAll` ○ `acUp` searches back through the records from the start point. The default setting is `acSearchAll`
`Searchasformatted`	Use `True` to search for data as it is formatted and `False` to search for data as it is stored in the database. The default is `False`.
`Onlycurrentfield`	If you leave this argument blank, the default constant (`acCurrent`) is assumed.
`Start from`	Setting this to True will force the search to start from record number 1 each time. This is the default record. `False` will start from the record following the current record.

Acceptance testing   152, 163–4
Access   107, 117
Adaptive maintenance   165
Algorithms   144–5
Alice's chocolate project   60–74, 193–8
Alice's chocolates stock control system
        117–23, 210–11
Analysis   125–6, 135–40, 176, 179
Annotation   167
Appraisal   128, 161, 176–8, 181
Archive system   178
Arithmetic buttons   23–4
Assignment   21
Attribute names   107

Background information   135
Basic calculator   19–27
Beginners All-purpose Symbolic
        Instruction Code *see* BASIC
Black box testing   152
Borders   64
Boundary data   152
Breakpoints   47
Button bars   4

Calculator   19–27, 184–6
Captions   14, 29
Car hire project   28–34, 187
Carriage return/line feed   58
Case statements   42
Case study   129–30
Character count   150
Check boxes   4, 8, 79, 82
Chris' car customiser project   75–97,
        199–205
Clear command   2
Clear key   22
Code listing   167, 183–211
Combo boxes   8, 30–2
Command buttons   4, 8, 13, 85, 108
    adding code   16–17, 109
Commenting   167–8
Commenting code   48

Common dialog boxes   89–90
Constants   148
Context diagrams   139
Control arrays   37, 40–2
Control name prefixes   212
Controls   4
Conventions   2
Corrective maintenance   165
Coursework   125–82
    analysis   125–6, 135–40
    appraisal   128, 161, 176–8
    assessment   128–9, 158–9
    system design   126, 141–6
    system maintenance   127–8, 165–71
    system testing   127, 160–4
    technical solution   126–7, 158–9
    user manual   128, 172–5

Data capture boxes   4
Data entry   149–50
Data Flow Diagrams (DFDs)   137,
        139–40, 179
Data requirements   146–53, 180
Data structures   146–7
Data types   146
Database   117–18, 159
Dates   55, 95, 146
Debugging   46–9
Declaration   23
Design   98–9, 126, 141–5, 180
    user interface   154–7
DFDs *see* Data Flow Diagrams
Dialog boxes   89–90
Dimension   23
Directory structure   87
Do/loop until   57
DoCmd   215
Documentation   127, 136–7, 158,
        179–81
Drop-down lists   4

Error trapping   25–7
Errors   17, 73

Excel 107
Executable files 18

Fatal errors 26
Feasibility study 137, 179
Files 3, 147, 167
Focus 73
Fonts 93
For/next loops 83, 88
Form designs 154–6, 180
Format check 150
Formatting 49
Formatting numbers 33–4, 44–5
Forms 3–4, 6, 148, 169–70
Frames 77
Fruit selector project 98–106, 206–7
Functional testing 152

General objectives 138
getting started 5–6
Global variables 63
Graphical User Interface (GUI) 3
GUI *see* Graphical User Interface

Handles 10
HCI *see* Human computer interface
Hot-keys 16
Human computer interface (HCI) 98,
    155

If/then statements 81
ImageFolder 98
Improvements 178
Input masks 150
Installation 173–4
Integers 146
Integrity 151
Interviews 135–6
Invalid data 152
Invoice creator 35–45, 188–9
Iterative processes 43, 66

Jack's garage project 50–9, 190–2

Jackson Structured Programming (JSP)
    142
JSP *see* Jackson Structured
    Programming

Kill 96

Labels 4, 8
Layout 14–16
Limitations 139
List box 8
Local variables 63
Look-up check 150
Loops 43

Menu buttons 85
Message boxes 68, 213–14
Methods 5–6
Modular structure 144
Modules 64, 166–7

Naming conventions 49
Nesting 58
Null value 112
Numeric buttons 21

Objectives 138
Observation 136
Open-source code 127
Option buttons 8, 77–8
Outputs 170

Passwords 151
Perfective maintenance 165
Prefixes 10, 212
Presence check 150
Printed outputs 157, 180
Printing 92–3
Procedures 144, 166–7
Programming VB 3–123
Project Explorer 4, 7
Project ideas 131–4
Project life cycle 125–30

Projects 3
Properties 4–5, 9, 20
    changing 12

Questionnaires 135–6
Quotes 76

Random access file 61
Random number generator 103
Random numbers 101–3
Range check 150
Read-only files 151
Real 23
Record navigation 113
Records 51–4, 146–7
Recovery plans 151
Refresh 67
Reserved name 55

Sample error message 175
Save 12
Scroll bars 4
Search 56, 110–12
Security 151
Serial files 50, 54
Single stepping 47–8
Source code 127
Specific objectives 138
Specifications 76
spell-check window 4
Splash screens 155
String 23, 61, 146
Structure diagrams 142–3
Sub-forms 3–4, 6
Sub-routines 144
Switchboard 155
Syntax 121
System design 126, 141–5, 180
System flowchart 141–2, 171
System maintenance 127–8, 158,
    165–71, 181
System testing 127, 152, 160–4, 180

Systems constants 68

Tab stops 73–4
Technical solution 126–7, 158–9, 180
Test strategies 151–3
Testing 24–7, 49
Text boxes 4, 8, 11
Text editor 10–18, 183
Timer 105
Toolbox 8, 108
Type check 149

Underscore 2
Unit testing 152
User feedback 176–7
User interface 22, 63, 104–5, 154–7, 180
User interview 135–6
User manual 128, 172–5, 181
User-defined variables 63–4

Validation 146–53, 180
Variable watching 47–8
Variables 22, 148, 165–6
    basic calculator 23
    fruit selector project 100–1
    invoice creator 39–40
    random access files 63
VB = Visual Basic
VBA *see* Visual Basic for Applications
versions of VB 1
Video hire shop project 107–16,
    208–10
View Code 6, 7
View Object 6, 7
Visual Basic for Applications (VBA)
    code 121
    stock control project 117–23
    video shop project 107–16

White box testing 152
Windows 3
    see also forms